ILLYRIA

ILLYRIA

A Play in Three Scenes

RICHARD NELSON

THEATRE COMMUNICATIONS GROUP
NEW YORK
2019

Illyria is published by Theatre Communications Group, Inc.,
520 Eighth Avenue, 24th Floor, New York, NY 10018-4156

The publication of *Illyria* by Richard Nelson, through TCG's Book Program, is made possible in part by the New York State Council on the Arts with the support of Governor Andrew Cuomo and the New York State Legislature.

TCG books are exclusively distributed to the book trade by Consortium Book Sales and Distribution.

Library of Congress Control Numbers:
2019034368 (print) / 2019034369 (ebook)
ISBN 978-1-55936-592-5 (paperback) / ISBN 978-1-55936-908-4 (ebook)
A catalog record for this book is available from the Library of Congress.

Book design and composition by Lisa Govan
Cover design by Mark Melnick
Cover photograph: Central Park, c. 1950s. Photographer unknown.
Courtesy of TimeFreezePhotos.com

First Edition, October 2019

For Rob

———

CONTENTS

FOREWORD

By Robert Marx

THE OPENING NIGHT of *Illyria* at The Public Theater was a site-specific occasion.

In the audience were many people old enough to have known nearly all the play's real-life characters—most crucially Joseph Papp, founder of The Public Theater (which still operates legally with the name Papp gave it, "The New York Shakespeare Festival"). Peggy Papp, Bernard Gersten, and David Amram were there, watching themselves depicted as they were almost six decades earlier, in 1958. Miranda Papp, the daughter of Joe and Peggy and an offstage character in *Illyria*, was also at the performance, as actors portrayed her parents' marriage just a year after her birth.

Richard Nelson has always been a master of irony and character contradiction, but this performance (to echo the title of a very early Nelson drama) conjured an event. Seated on three sides around the same thrust stage that opened The Public Theater in 1967, the audience wasn't always sure what to watch: the actor playing Bernie Gersten, or Bernie Gersten watching that actor play him. And then, cutting across so much of the opening night audience, were our individual memories of Joe and Bernie and Merle and Colleen and the building itself; our own time spent there; decades of experiences with Joe both searing and wonderful, on stage and off, with hirings and firings that shaped careers and lives. It was a complicated evening.

Ironies were layered upon ironies, the greatest being that the scrappy, homeless, almost improvisational theater depicted in *Illyria* soon became (and still is) one of the institutional powerhouses of American theater. The other, more established, financially stable and prominent theaters of 1958 that are argued over in *Illyria* would all eventually close. It was Papp's itinerant enterprise that took root—the one where there was no money for a second copy of *Twelfth Night*, or even a level stage on which to perform. Just four years after the events depicted in *Illyria*, New York City would build Papp a two-thousand-seat summer theater for free Shakespeare in Central Park, followed by the historic Astor Library's conversion into The Public Theater as his multistage home for new plays. The rain did not raineth every day. The bricks-and-mortar of *Illyria*'s theater and its opening night audience were living proof of that.

But *Illyria* is not an event-driven celebration of Papp and his legacy. It's a play of anger and arguments that subtly raises questions about American theater today, in the early twenty-first century. Descending from this historic *Illyria* in Central Park, what makes a "real" theater, now, for us? Is a theater a building, or its people?

The characters of Nelson's New York Shakespeare Festival are full of painful doubt and insecurity, arguing about what makes that "real" theater: one that supports careers, or one that's "not about anything but doing it," as Peggy Papp says, somewhat forlornly, in the play's final scene. Between those two extremes lie all the contradictions of young theater lives.

How can the grinding need to earn a living and the idealist need to make a difference be reconciled? What is art and what is profit? And who is it all for?

As in many of Nelson's dramas, class issues slice through his characters. In *Illyria*, Joe Papp has jealous contempt for his well-funded rivals, the Phoenix Theatre (based in a refurbished Yiddish playhouse on Second Avenue), the large-scale summer Shakespeare festivals in Stratford (both Connecticut and Canada), and the not-yet-built "culture palace" that will become Lincoln Center. Papp's artistic director, Stuart Vaughan, jumps to the Phoenix, setting off a crisis among friends, a group under constant pressure not only to abandon "Free Shakespeare," but their basic working lives and beliefs amid the McCarthy blacklisting era.

At *Illyria*'s core, the raging argument about the New York Shakespeare Festival that breaks out between Papp and Vaughan is a quintessential Richard Nelson dialogue. Complex truths and contradictions converge from both sides. Uncertainties don't resolve, but expand. Individual choices affect everyone, and those choices define lives. Amid their fury over opportunity and obligation, where is the moral compass, not just for theater people, but for theaters?

Lurking beneath the arguments fought by *Illyria*'s young theater crowd is a potent historical observation. In 1958, there was still a strong connection between New York City's working-class population and its theaters—not just the audience, but the people who work in theater. Theater tickets were comparatively cheap. A rear balcony seat in a Broadway house was the price of a movie. Off-Broadway tickets were even less. And Papp (inspired by the New York Public Library) took the next step, making tickets free. There was a marketing line in vogue then, "The *Times* sells the orchestra, but the *Daily News* sells the balcony." The economic diversity that was still so much a part of theater audiences in 1958 is gone today. In many ways, those early park audiences for Papp were the backbone of all New York theater, but by the 1980s, economic forces and profit-taking would exclude them, to be replaced largely by tourist dollars. Taking stock of that retrenchment, *Illyria* turns away from the high-end institutional assumptions that control American theater now. It points toward "the doing of it" in the mission-based terms of a young Joe Papp, who at the time of this play was not all that far from the dire poverty of his Brooklyn childhood.

It's often said that we can't re-create Joe Papp, because the American society he emerged from is gone. Certainly, that's true. And in contemporary terms it's hard to convey the kind of forceful, strong-armed leader Papp became in the 1960s and 1970s; a man who absolutely dominated New York theater, becoming a virtually unchallenged national symbol.

New York theater is a different place without him and his kind. Where today are dedicated producers of scorching public nerve and authority who push the art of theater on their own terms? Producers who out of dedication and commitment set productions before the public for no reason other than their unshakable belief in a play or performance? Where are producers who truly lead the profession, defying self-authorized censors and politicians in the faith that theater should be new and uncomfortable and just possibly free, and absolutely without borders or blacklists? Who among today's producers would stand before bulldozers rather than see even one more theater building fall to "progress"?

There were others at the time, people Papp often viewed as rivals, but who were as passionate in their commitments to playwrights, actors, directors, and stage designers. (Lucille Lortel and T. Edward Hambleton used their personal fortunes not only to produce plays, but help people's lives offstage, including many blacklisted artists. Ellen Stewart of La MaMa, who rose from poverty and oppression even greater than what Papp faced, became a sui generis world figure supporting American experimental theater.) In all, they defined the best of a community run by individuals, made by hand,

and ruled by loyalty and devotion. Looking back, they were a group of supreme theater people who in different ways did their jobs well, who showed us how the work could be done. They were producers motivated by art and its role in society, never greed, and always with a conviction that theater is important. Fundamentally so.

The theater world of Joe Papp may seem very distant now, but one of *Illyria*'s virtues is that it makes us look back at a time when theater was bursting in unprecedented directions, reinventing itself in what was still the postwar landscape. Aside from the New York Shakespeare Festival and the Phoenix, there was La MaMa, Caffe Cino, the Living Theatre, the Judson Poets Theater, Circle in the Square, Theatre Genesis, and so many more stages exploding inherited assumptions about new plays and classics. The American regional theater movement was just taking off. Zelda Fichandler was already hurling radical manifestos at her audiences in Washington. In London, the Royal Shakespeare Company and the National Theatre would soon be launched with intense rivalry. After that came the Théâtre du Soleil in Paris and the Schaubühne in Berlin—all young theaters, and totally distinct from each other. Theater was hot, and stayed that way for decades.

Ultimately, *Illyria* looks forward, not back, suggesting that the questions asked by Nelson's struggling characters in Central Park must be repeated today, and with greater force. In our time, there is a need to reinvent the assumptions and goals of theater producing, just as Papp did. His own generation fled commercial theater to create not-for-profits, and now, a half-century later, a new crowd may have to escape from those often-hidebound institutions for something as radical in contemporary terms as what Papp and co. envisioned in the 1950s.

The New York Shakespeare Festival of *Illyria* is a stand-in for all ambitious, defiant and obsessed young theaters. It's an invention of confusion, anger, doubt, and talent set long ago, but meant to challenge everyone who comes after not to dream and do as well as, but better—to defy and improve and rejoice on their own living stage.

New York City
October 2019

ROBERT MARX is president of the Fan Fox and Leslie R. Samuels Foundation in New York City. Since the 1970s, he has worked throughout the United States and abroad as an essayist, producer and consultant in theater and opera.

ILLYRIA

———

Illyria was originally developed and produced by The Public Theater (Oskar Eustis, Artistic Director; Patrick Willingham, Executive Director) in New York, on October 29, 2017. It was directed by Richard Nelson. The scenic design was by Susan Hilferty and Jason Ardizzone-West, the costume design was by Susan Hilferty, the lighting design was by Jennifer Tipton and the sound design was by Scott Lehrer. The production stage manager was Jared Oberholtzer and the production manager was Jeff Harris. The cast was:

JOE PAPP	John Magaro
PEGGY PAPP	Kristen Connolly
MERLE DEBUSKEY	Fran Kranz
STUART VAUGHAN	John Sanders
GLADYS VAUGHAN	Emma Duncan
DAVID AMRAM	Blake DeLong
JOHN ROBERTSON	Max Woertendyke
BERNIE GERSTEN	Will Brill
MARY BENNETT	Naian González Norvind
COLLEEN DEWHURST	Rosie Benton

CHARACTERS

JOE PAPP, producer, the Shakespeare Festival, thirty-seven

PEGGY PAPP, his wife, an actress, thirty-five

MERLE DEBUSKEY, press agent for the festival, thirty-eight

STUART VAUGHAN, director for the festival, thirty-three

GLADYS VAUGHAN, his wife, Joe's assistant, thirty

DAVID AMRAM, musician and composer, twenty-eight

JOHN ROBERTSON, stage manager, twenty-six

BERNIE GERSTEN, Joe's friend, a stage manager, thirty-five

MARY BENNETT, an actress, twenty-four

COLLEEN DEWHURST, an actress, thirty-four

TIME AND PLACE

The play takes place between April and August, 1958; New York City.

Scene 1:
April; Greenroom, Heckscher Auditorium, Fifth Avenue and 104th Street. 1:30 P.M.

Scene 2:
June 22; Colleen's apartment, Upper West Side. Early afternoon.

Scene 3:
August; temporary stage, Belvedere lawn, Central Park. Night.

PUNCTUATION

Double quotation marks are used when someone is reading from something or directly quoting. Single quotation marks are used when someone is paraphrasing or generalizing.

Dialogue in brackets is unspoken.

Scene 1

Greenroom. Heckscher Auditorium, Fifth Avenue and 104th Street. April, 1958. A large table; a few wooden chairs and folding chairs, a side table with an electric coffee percolator and mugs; a couple of stained, maybe broken, armchairs; rugs, a piano, coffee table. A typical greenroom. It is after a student matinee.

    Mary and Stuart have been waiting; she holds a paperback copy of Twelfth Night; *he has been looking through his mail. John has just entered and is pouring himself a cup of coffee.*

MARY: He tells you to start the play?

JOHN: Joe orders me to start the goddamn play. "Jacques isn't on for a while," he says, and he's sure Scott will be here any second now.

MARY: You don't have understudies?

STUART *(Of course not)*: No.

(David enters with his guitar.)

JOHN: I'm telling them about our fun morning, David.

DAVID: Fucking George Scott.

STUART: Gladys already told me some of it.

JOHN: We'd already held for maybe twenty-five minutes.

DAVID: Felt like three hours.

JOHN: And the kids were going crazy. David, my hero, went out onstage alone, and played songs for the kids.

DAVID: No one listened. They were screaming. They're kids at a student matinee.

(John hands David a coffee.)

Thanks.

JOHN: I do what I'm told and call 'places,' with no Jacques. We finish the first act: no Jacques. We get all the way into the second act: no Jacques. We're two pages before his entrance, I look to Joe who's with me in the wings, and Joe just walks away. We have no Jacques. When suddenly Scott comes running through the stage door. And I don't think he'd slept.

STUART: Gladys said hungover.

JOHN: Or still drunk. That's what Gladys said to me. She got close to him. She smelled him. *(To Mary)* He's growling . . . Growling at everyone.

STUART *(To David)*: Or is that his 'acting'?

DAVID: You directed him.

STUART: No one directs him.

JOHN: Scott grabs half his costume— He's still in one of his street shoes . . .

DAVID: He's still got his watch on. He's fucking Jacques. Jacques with a goddamn Timex.

JOHN: And then, like that, Scott is—on.

DAVID: In the forest of Arden. There's a look in his eye: 'Where am I?' Silence. And one kid suddenly shouts out some stupid thing. I couldn't even hear what he shouted . . .

JOHN: I think he shouted, "Hey mister, why do you have your watch on?"

STUART: Fucking unbelievable.

JOHN: And I guess Scott has heard this, because now dressed as—I don't know what he was dressed as—he's got this huge turkey leg in his hand, that's his prop—every day we have to get him a new one—

STUART: Because he eats it, John.

JOHN (*Over this*): —he barges out into the audience of schoolkids, now very frightened-looking schoolkids. He finds *the* kid who shouted, thinks he's found *the* kid, maybe it wasn't even the right kid, I don't know, he doesn't know, and he looks down at this tiny little kid, leans down, so they're face to face now, and he screams at the top of his lungs: "Will you shut the fuck up!"

MARY: Where were the teachers?

JOHN: They're out having a goddamn smoke, Mary.

STUART: The teachers are the worst.

MARY: Are they?

JOHN: Some of them. Joe says we should just hire Scott out to the schools. He'd get them to behave. They were all quiet after that.

STUART: I'll bet.

DAVID: They were scared.

JOHN: Yeah . . . They were. (*Just realizing, to David and Mary*) You two haven't met.

DAVID: We haven't.

MARY (*Same*): No.

JOHN: David—Mary. Mary—David.

DAVID: How do you do? John's told me all about you.

MARY: And you. Nice to meet you.

JOHN (*To Mary*): You all right?

MARY: Just waiting.

STUART (*To David*): Do you know where Joe is?

DAVID: Probably still with Gladys, trying to herd Scott back into his dressing room.

STUART *(To John)*: Is there any more coffee? I was up early.

JOHN: I just finished it.

MARY: What were you going to do if he didn't show up?

(John shrugs.)

I'm amazed you can talk about it so . . .

JOHN: What?

MARY: Calmly. If I'd just—

JOHN: I'm a stage manager. I'm always calm.

MARY: Not at home you're not. He's not.

DAVID: What's John like at home, Mary?

JOHN: Shut up, David.

MARY *(Again)*: What were you going to do?

JOHN: I was getting ready to read his fucking lines.

MARY: You're a terrible actor.

JOHN: They're kids, Mary.

DAVID *(To Mary)*: When have you seen John act? *(To Stuart)* Have you ever seen him act?

STUART *(To Mary)*: He 'acts' for you?

MARY: Sometimes he reads lines with me. When I'm learning a role—

DAVID: He 'acts' for her, Stuart.

JOHN: Shut up.

DAVID: She's blushing.

MARY: I am not blushing. Why do you say that?

JOHN: Come on.

DAVID *('Innocently')*: What?

JOHN *(To Mary)*: Ignore them.

STUART: What's John like at home, Mary? Tell us. *(To David, snapping his fingers)* He's a stage manager. Cue. Cue cue. Cue.

DAVID *(Still teasing John, to Stuart, about his 'cueing')*: Cue! That's him in bed.

STUART: David . . .

JOHN *(About Stuart and David)*: They *are* grown-ups. Sometimes. They can be. You'll have to trust me. *(Back to the story)* Stuart, while I was standing outside looking up and down the street for George Scott, I hear one teacher tell another—"I'm on my way to that bar over on Lex."

DAVID *(To Mary)*: They abandon us. Joe says, they treat it like it's a big goddamn vacation for them—a student matinee.

JOHN *(Repeats)*: Some of them.

STUART *(To Mary)*: They abandon us. You go out there on a student matinee, you know you're on your own.

DAVID: You weren't even there, Stuart.

(Gladys, thirty, Stuart's wife and Joe's assistant, enters.)

GLADYS: John . . .

JOHN: So where's Scott now?

GLADYS: He wants a cab. Can you do that, John? Please. I think I've had enough of him for one day.

JOHN *(Getting up)*: Where is he?

GLADYS: Dressing room. Joe's babysitting. He's telling Joe stories. George Scott always has lots of stories. I think he thinks he's still in a bar.

JOHN: That little kid'll have nightmares for years. *(To Mary)* Good luck . . .

MARY: Thanks.

GLADYS: What was he thinking, John?

(John heads off.)

"Little boy, will you shut the fuck up"?? They're children.

(She has looked toward the coffee pot.)

DAVID: There's no more coffee.

STUART *(Introducing)*: Gladys—Mary Bennett.

GLADYS *(Shaking hands)*: How do you do?

STUART *(To David)*: Scott's still worth the trouble though, don't you think?

DAVID: I suppose so . . .

STUART: We're talking about doing something else.

DAVID: Are you?

GLADYS *(Same time)*: You told me.

STUART: Sometimes he can be brilliant.

GLADYS: I know.

STUART: Mary, Scott does the seven ages of man speech—?

MARY: I know the speech.

STUART: That can be brilliant.

DAVID: Was that your idea?

STUART: Some of it.

MARY: What?

DAVID: George eats a great big turkey leg while giving the speech. *(Smiles)* Every day John has to buy—

MARY: He said.

DAVID: So each "age of man" it's like—rip. *(Rips with his teeth)* And then . . . And then . . .

STUART *(Over this)*: He's supposed to take just one bite, not . . .

DAVID: Stuart, this morning—

STUART: What did he do this morning?

DAVID: He was probably very hungry, probably hadn't had breakfast. Maybe dinner. And he ate his turkey leg with so much goddamn relish—it was almost obscene.

MARY: Was it?

DAVID: Juice running down his chin . . . I think that's what scared the girls in the uniforms.

STUART: Catholic schoolgirls?

DAVID: They got all quiet in an odd sort of way . . .

STUART: Jesus. Still when he's good, there's no one better. We're talking about a few things he could play. Good parts.

DAVID: I thought he wanted to do movies.

STUART: He might do a movie. But it's 'iffy.'

DAVID: Aren't movies always 'iffy'?

STUART *(Shrugs)*: He talks. I let him talk. He belongs in the theater. And if he does get a movie, we can work around that. It's not like in the park . . . *(The third time he's asked, to Mary)* When do you have to be back?

MARY: I've missed the lunch crowd. *(Shrugs)* I'm fine. David, I waited on George Scott once . . . He's a good tipper.

STUART: Actors often are. *(To Gladys)* Can you go and remind Joe that we're waiting?

GLADYS: I'll go tell him . . .

(She heads off.
David peeks at Mary's book.)

DAVID: *Twelfth Night.* So we're doing that next?

MARY: You didn't know that you're—?

STUART: Don't believe anything David says to you. And David will say a lot to someone like you.

MARY: What do you mean—someone like me?

DAVID *(To 'Stuart')*: Why does our stage manager get to have such a beautiful girlfriend?

STUART: Like that. He'll say things like that.

DAVID *(To Mary, 'incredulous')*: And we've never met. You're sure about that?

STUART: And that.

MARY *('Answering')*: Maybe. You look a little familiar.

STUART: She'll be a very good Olivia.

MARY: I hope you're still saying that after I've auditioned . . .

DAVID *(Teasing her)*: I could play while you . . .

STUART: David.

DAVID: Something like . . .

(He plays the guitar.)

STUART *(Over this)*: Leave Mary alone. Don't bother her.

DAVID: I'm not—

MARY: He isn't . . .

(David strums.)

STUART *(To Mary)*: When I saw you in *Merry Wives* I hadn't
    realized, you and John . . . He's a very good stage manager.
MARY: I'm sure he is.
DAVID: He's very clean. Very neat. Good with the 'cues,' right?
MARY *(Smiling)*: Really good.
STUART: John's a friend of ours. Isn't he, David? And *this* is his
    girlfriend . . .
MARY *(Smiling)*: I am.
STUART *(To Mary)*: I hate pretty much everything I see up in
    Stratford. *(To David)* Can you stop playing that? *(To Mary)*
    I mean, you have to almost kidnap me to get me on that
    train to Stratford. Because I know what will be awaiting at
    the end of the road.
MARY: What is?
STUART: Stratford. *(About Mary)* So—I was very pleasantly
    surprised.
DAVID: I've never worked there. I've tried . . .
STUART: They're not going to hire you. People like us, we scare
    them in Stratford.
DAVID: She works there, Stuart.
MARY: Once. But I agree, it's awful there. Like a factory. But
    I'll work anywhere.

(Gladys returns.)

STUART: So where the hell is Joe?
GLADYS: Merle just arrived. Now they're talking.
STUART: Oh please . . . Come on. I told this young woman one
    o'clock.
MARY: I'm in no hurry. I'm okay. I have nothing to do. I already
    missed the lunch crowd.
GLADYS *(To Stuart)*: We doing this onstage?

STUART: It's fine here, isn't it? *(To Mary)* This okay? We don't need to be onstage. It's always too—'formal' onstage. I hate that. *(Looks to Mary)*

MARY: Anything . . .

DAVID *(Standing up)*: Should I—?

STUART: Stay. He could be forever with Merle. *(As David sits back down, about Mary)* I didn't have to ask you twice.

MARY: 'What?'

STUART *('Calls')*: John!

MARY: He's busy.

GLADYS: I hope he's getting George into a cab. Please god . . .

STUART *(To David)*: Let her prepare.

GLADYS: Did you see those teachers outside? What are we now, babysitters? Joe was furious. He's going to write a letter. He's asked me to write a letter. *(To Stuart)* She's reading Olivia?

STUART: She is.

GLADYS: My husband is a fan, I understand.

STUART: I certainly am.

GLADYS: We saw you at Stratford. I love going there. I love the country. Where do you want Mary?

(He points.)

STUART: And Joe and I . . .

(He points—behind the table.)

GLADYS: And I should read with her?

STUART: Please. Thank you, Gladys.

DAVID *(A 'wink' at Mary)*: Or maybe John should.

(Mary smiles.)

Make you look good.

GLADYS: What are you talking about?? Are you staying, David? Don't you have to—?

MARY: I don't mind if he stays.

(David has started to stand.)

I'd sort of like an audience. It makes it easier for some reason.

GLADYS *(To Stuart)*: Is that all right?

STUART *(To David)*: Stay. Stay . . . This won't take long. She's really good . . .

GLADYS: I know.

STUART *(To David)*: You want to go out after . . . ? And talk? Maybe go to the movies? *(To Gladys)* David told me yesterday that he's interested in the Phoenix.

GLADYS: Why am I not surprised?

DAVID: I've wanted to ask how much are they paying? Are *you* paying, I should say? Now that it's you. *(To Mary)* He's now a boss.

MARY: I know. I just read that.

STUART: I don't know, David. But it's a real theater. So real pay. *(To Mary)* I don't mean to say this [here]—

MARY: I understand.

STUART: —isn't.

DAVID: We're 'real,' aren't we?

GLADYS: I think so.

STUART *(Over this)*: So I assume—real proper pay. T and I haven't discussed salaries yet. Even for composers. Musicians.

DAVID: That'll be a change.

STUART *(Over this)*: T has money. *That* you figure out right away.

GLADYS *(To Mary)*: Is this your copy?

MARY: It is . . .

STUART *(To Gladys)*: Do we have another copy?

DAVID: Of *Twelfth Night?* We should, we're a Shakespeare festival.

GLADYS: I don't think we do. I just looked.

STUART: There's not another copy?

DAVID *(Over this, to Stuart, trying to make a joke)*: I'll bet Stratford has two copies of *Twelfth Night.*

STUART *(Over this, a joke)*: I'll make it a policy to have at least *two* copies of any play we do at the Phoenix.

GLADYS *(To Mary)*: What if I read over your shoulder? Will that bother you?

MARY: I don't think so. No.

DAVID: Mary, which one is Olivia, I always get them mixed up?

GLADYS: Not the one who wears pants, David.

(As Joe and Merle enter:)

JOE: Here they are, Merle. Why aren't we on the stage? We were just looking for you on the stage.

GLADYS: We thought it'd be less formal, Joe. Relaxed . . .

STUART: You want to go up on the stage?

JOE: We thought you'd left . . . .

STUART: Why would I leave?

JOE: I just didn't know where you were.

GLADYS: You want to do this up—?

JOE: This is fine. Whatever.

STUART: Joe, this is Mary Bennett.

JOE *(Shaking hands)*: Hello.

MERLE *(Shaking hands)*: Hi. Merle . . .

STUART *(For the fifth time)*: I've seen her work. In Stratford. *Merry Wives* . . .

JOE: I thought you never went to Stratford.

GLADYS: I dragged him.

JOE *(To Stuart)*: They're not going to hire you. I've told you that.

(As Merle looks toward the coffee pot:)

STUART: There's no more coffee.

JOE: Is there enough room here? We have a big stage.

STUART: It's fine, Joe.

GLADYS *(To Joe)*: She's going to be there. I'm reading with her.

JOE *(To Mary)*: I think I've seen your work too . . .

MARY: In what, Mr. Papp?

JOE: Weren't you in a class with my wife? Or am I wrong? Was that someone else?

MARY: I was in an acting class with Peggy . . . Last year. In the fall.

JOE: Then I saw you there. I thought you looked familiar.

STUART: Then you've met . . . Good. That's good.

JOE: Nice to see you again, Mary. And thank you so much for coming in. For taking the time. I'm very sorry if we've kept you waiting. It's been an interesting morning, Mary. *(This explains everything)* Scott.

MARY: It's no problem . . .

JOE: You in something now?

MARY: Not right now, no, sir.

JOE *(To Gladys)*: She'll be there? I'm here?

MERLE: Joe, should I—go?

STUART: This won't take long. She said she likes an audience, Merle. *(To Mary)* Didn't you?

JOE: That's lucky. For you. Being an actress . . .

(Smiles at his joke.)

Mary, you weren't by any chance in the audience this morning?

STUART: She wasn't, Joe.

DAVID: We were just telling her about that.

JOE: He made a little boy cry, Mary.

STUART: So—should we start?

JOE: We have kept this woman waiting long enough.

(Arranging themselves:)

(To Merle) Sit by me. Sit here. Congratulations, Stuart. I don't think I've congratulated you.

STUART: Actually you have.

MERLE *(Taking a seat, to Stuart)*: Congratulations.

STUART: Thank you.

JOE *(To Merle)*: Stuart's got a new job.

MERLE: We all know that, Joe.

JOE: He doesn't look any different.

STUART *(For the tenth time, over this)*: And it doesn't affect anything with the festival.

JOE *(Confused)*: Is David playing during this?

DAVID: I'm not. Want me to go?

JOE *(To Stuart)*: I thought you had some fancy 'director's idea' for the part. *(Smiles)* That you hadn't told me about.

STUART: I don't.

JOE: What is she reading for?

(This takes Stuart aback.)

STUART: 'Olivia,' Joe. You know that.

JOE: 'Olivia.' Right. You want me to read with her?

GLADYS: I'm reading with her.

JOE: Just want to help.

GLADYS *(Quietly to Mary)*: Where are we starting?

MARY: Stuart told me here . . .

(She points to the place in the book.)

JOE: David, did you see the paper this morning? What's he talking about?

DAVID: I haven't. Who?

JOE: Kerr.

MERLE: We're going to write him, Joe.

JOE: What the hell is he talking about? And why is it his business?

MERLE: I've tried to explain it to him, Joe; he's a little thick. He's a critic.

(They have all taken their seats, Mary at some distance from the others; Gladys behind her.)

GLADYS: Are we ready? *(To Stuart)* "Give me your hand, sir"?
STUART: From there's fine.

(Joe leans over to speak to Merle.)

JOE: We should write that letter—
STUART: Joe . . .
MERLE: I'll write him.

(Joe sits back to watch the audition. They read from Twelfth Night, *Act III, Scene i.)*

JOE *(To Stuart)*: I really meant it—congratulations.
MARY: May I stand, move around?
STUART: Of course.
GLADYS: I'll just follow . . . Anytime . . .
JOE *(To Stuart)*: T. Hambleton's one lucky man.
STUART: Thank you.
MARY: Now? *(Reading, though she has it mostly memorized)*

Give me your hand, sir.

GLADYS:
My duty, madam, and most humble service.

MARY:
What is your name?

JOE: Don't we have another copy?
STUART: Sh-sh . . . It's fine.
DAVID *(Over this)*: We don't.
GLADYS *(Quietly to Mary)*: Let's start again . . .

MARY:
Give me your hand, sir.

GLADYS:
My duty, madam, and most humble service.

MARY:

> What is your name?

GLADYS:

> Cesario is your servant's name, fair princess.

MARY:

> My servant, sir? 'Twas never merry world
> Since lowly feigning was called compliment.
> Y'are servant to the Count Orsino, youth.

GLADYS:

> And he is yours, and his must needs be yours.
> Your servant's servant is your servant, madam.

MARY:

> For him, I think not on him; for his thoughts,
> Would they were blanks, rather than filled with me.

GLADYS:

> Madam, I come to whet your gentle thoughts
> On his behalf.

MARY:

> O, by your leave, I pray you.
> I bade you never speak again to him;
> But, would you undertake another suit,
> I had rather hear you to solicit that
> Than music from the spheres . . .

JOE *(Stopping her)*: Very nice, Mary. Really nice.
> Thank, you . . . That's all I think we need, isn't it, Stuart?
MARY *(To Gladys, over this)*: We're stopping?
GLADYS *(Confused)*: I guess so . . .
JOE *(Quotes)*: ". . . for his thoughts, / Would they were blanks,
rather than filled with me." I love that line.

STUART *(Confused)*: Joe, she just started—

JOE: She's very good Stuart. You're right. She deserves better than Stratford. Thank you, Mary. What was it you read in Peggy's class? Juliet, I think.

STUART: Joe?

MARY: I did do Juliet . . .

JOE: I remember your Juliet. You're very good.

GLADYS *(To Stuart)*: Is that all you need?

STUART: I don't know.

MARY: Is that all . . . ?

GLADYS: I think it is. I think so.

JOE: I'm good. I know the work, Stuart.

STUART: I hadn't realized Joe knew your work.

MARY *(To Gladys)*: You don't need to hear—?

GLADYS: No. I don't think so. I think that's all we need right now.

STUART: We seem to be happy. Am I right?

JOE *(A joke)*: You're too good for Stratford.

STUART: I think we'll be able to let you know very soon. So— that's it. I guess . . . Joe?

JOE: I know her work.

GLADYS *(A sweater)*: Is this yours, Mary?

(As Mary collects her things:)

MARY: I seem to have left my stuff all over . . .

GLADYS: Take your time . . . No rush. Can I help . . . ?

MARY: Thanks. Sorry . . . Thank you . . . Sorry . . .

JOE: Merle, I think I've now got Scott to agree to play Iago for us this summer.

MERLE: That's good news.

GLADYS: You're sure he agreed? He's hoping for a movie, I heard.

JOE: He's agreed. Merle, George was just telling me that Stuart's talking to him about doing something at the Phoenix. *(To Stuart)* You can't steal everyone away, Stuart.

STUART *(For the tenth time)*: I'm not trying to, Joe . . .

(As Mary picks up the last of her stuff:)

(To Mary) Thank you. Thanks. We should be able to let you
know very soon. We won't keep you waiting, I promise . . .
JOE: Mary, our stage manager is just in the hallway. He can
you show you out. It's a bit of a rabbit's warren down here.
Introduce yourself . . .
DAVID: They live together, Joe.
JOE: What? Who?
DAVID: Robertson and Mary. They live together.
JOE: Do you? You and John? Really?

(He looks to Gladys who nods.)

Why didn't I know that? Thank you, Mary. Very nice.
Really nice . . .
MARY: I love the part . . . I'd love to do it.

(She goes.)

JOE *(To Merle)*: John and . . . John's a very good stage manager.
Don't you steal him, Stuart.
STUART: I can stop her. Should we stop her? She'll be great.
JOE: We'll talk . . .
STUART: What's there to talk about? We won't do any better.
GLADYS: Should I go get Peggy?
STUART *(Confused)*: What??
GLADYS: Peggy's here. She's in Joe's office. She's in there waiting.
JOE: She got a friend to babysit. That wasn't easy. She hardly
ever leaves the baby alone . . .
MERLE *(To Joe)*: She's two months old.
STUART: Why is Peggy here?
GLADYS: She wants to audition for you.
JOE *(To 'David')*: I keep telling her, she should get out. You stay
away too long and people forget what you've done.
STUART: Joe, Peggy doesn't have to audition for me.

JOE: That's what I told her. But you know Peggy . . . She wants to 'earn' it. Always has to do things right. *(To Gladys)* She told me last night that she's not even sure she wants to act anymore.

GLADYS: I know.

JOE: I told her, what a loss that would be. Then this morning, Stuart, she says: I know there's so much more to life than just being a mother . . . Back and forth. She goes back and forth . . . Gladys, I'll get her. She's nervous . . .

(Stands.)

And Stuart—I don't think she knows about—this Mary . . . That someone else . . .

GLADYS *(To Stuart)*: She wants to audition for Olivia.

JOE: So—you understand. Thanks.

(He goes.)

GLADYS: It's all right.

STUART: That son of a bitch. *(To Gladys)* Did you know about this?

GLADYS *(Over this)*: Stuart, just let her audition.

STUART: He knows I won't do this play with his wife.

GLADYS: If you've told him, then he knows. Calm down.

STUART: I've done five plays with his wife . . . We went through this last summer.

DAVID: Maybe she just wants to audition. An excuse to get out of the house.

STUART *(Again to Gladys)*: You knew about this.

GLADYS: You should have choices. You say that.

STUART: Shit . . .

(Joe and Peggy enter. He holds a couple of copies of Twelfth Night.*)*

JOE: Here she is . . .

STUART: Peggy . . .

PEGGY: It's a crowd . . . *(To David)* You're here too.

DAVID: Look at you. You look great. How's the baby?

PEGGY: She's beautiful, David.

(They hug.)

(To Joe) Isn't she beautiful?

MERLE: Miranda is a very beautiful child.

JOE: She's beautiful. So that's settled. *(Smiles)*

PEGGY: Stuart. Good to see you.

STUART: And you, Peggy. It's been a while.

(They hug.)

PEGGY: You should come over and see her.

STUART: I plan to, Peggy. I look forward to it.

PEGGY *(To Stuart)*: Merle's been.

STUART: I knew I wouldn't beat Merle.

MERLE: What does that mean?

(Peggy has started to sit at the table.)

GLADYS: Peggy, we'll be there . . .

PEGGY: Of course. It's been a while.

GLADYS: No, I didn't mean . . . When you're ready. And I'm
reading with you.

PEGGY: Good. *(To the others)* We've been rehearsing together.
I'm a little nervous, Stuart.

STUART *(Over this, to Gladys)*: Have you?

JOE *(Over this)*: And there's no reason to be. *(To Stuart)* Is there?
We're family . . .

PEGGY: Let's do this . . . *(Organizing herself, to Stuart)* Congratulations on the Phoenix. You got my note? Joe said
he'd give you my note . . .

JOE: I'll give it to you later. I have it in the office.

PEGGY: They're very lucky to have you. That's what I wrote. They got smart. Joe's jealous.

STUART: He shouldn't be.

PEGGY: Friends are saying they really hope they can audition now for things at the Phoenix. *(To Joe)* They can do both. No one's 'betraying' anything. I tell him *(Joe)* that.

STUART: Keep doing that. Please. Please.

JOE *(Holds up the copies of the play)*: We found our copies. Gladys . . .

(Gladys takes them from him, as:)

STUART: Are you all right doing this, Peggy? We all know your work so well.

PEGGY *(Repeats)*: It's been a while. We haven't done anything together for some time. Last summer, I knew I wasn't your idea of Kate. I'm not my idea of Kate. And you got Colleen so—and she was amazing. *(Smiles)* And it's just been so much fun rehearsing with your wife. I think I like the rehearsing part best. *(Smiles)*

GLADYS: The baby in one hand, the script in the other . . .

PEGGY: Not always. I'm afraid I'm a bit rusty.

JOE: It's been nearly a year—year and a half . . .

STUART: Gladys are we ready?

MERLE: You have somewhere to go?

JOE: She kept up with her classes . . . She still took classes. Even when— *(Gestures: pregnant)* David, put that down.

(David puts down his guitar.)

(To Peggy) I don't know how you did it. *(To Stuart)* She did a scene—the balcony scene in class—six months pregnant—

PEGGY: I had to stop the classes. I'm thinking of starting up again.

JOE *(To Merle, smiling)*: It was something to see.

MERLE: You told me. I would have liked to have seen that.

STUART: Anytime, Peggy. Gladys.

JOE *(To Stuart)*: Are we in a rush?

STUART *(Nods to David)*: We're going to the movies.

JOE: With him? *(To David)* You looking for a job too?

DAVID: We're going to the movies, Joe.

STUART: Gladys . . .

GLADYS *(To Peggy)*: You want to sit or stand?

PEGGY: I'll stand. Is that all right?

JOE: Of course . . .

GLADYS *(To Peggy)*: Stuart wants us starting—here I think . . .
Same place?

STUART: The same.

PEGGY: I know. Joe just told me.

JOE *(Leans over to Stuart)*: Give her suggestions, if you want.

STUART: We've worked together umpteen times.

JOE *(To Stuart)*: Tell her that she can move around . . . I didn't
think that other girl moved very well.

STUART: We didn't have two scripts.

PEGGY *(To Gladys)*: What other girl?

GLADYS: Go ahead . . . Go ahead . . .

PEGGY: I'm going to begin . . . *(Points)*

JOE *(To Merle)*: We worked on this . . .

PEGGY *(Reads)*:

> Let the garden door be shut, and leave me to my
>   hearing.
> Give me your hand, sir.

GLADYS:

> My duty, madam, and most humble service.

PEGGY:

> What is your name?

GLADYS:

> Cesario is your servant's name, fair princess.

PEGGY:

> My servant, sir? 'Twas never merry world
> Since lowly feigning was called compliment.
> Y' are servant to the Count Orsino, youth.

GLADYS:

> And he is yours, and his must needs be yours.
> Your servant's servant is your servant, madam.

PEGGY:

> For him, I think not on him; for his thoughts
> Would they were blanks, rather than filled with me.

GLADYS:

> Madam, I come to whet your gentle thoughts
> On his behalf.

PEGGY:

> O, by your leave, I pray you.
> I bade you never speak again of him;
> But, would you undertake another suit,
> I had rather hear you to solicit that
> Than the music from the spheres.

STUART *(Stopping her)*: Very nice, Peggy.

JOE: What are you doing?

STUART *(Over this)*: Really really nice. *(To Joe)* That's where we're stopping. *(To Peggy)* You don't seem rusty at all.

PEGGY *(Confused)*: Thanks.

STUART *(Over this)*: Thank you so much, Peggy. We know your work so well.

JOE: Stuart, what are you doing?

STUART *(Over this)*: Be quiet. I'm the director. I really appreciate you taking the time . . . We all know how difficult that is these days for you. Motherhood . . . Can you give us a day or two to decide?

PEGGY: Of course.

MERLE: You sure you've heard enough, Stuart?

STUART: I think it's really important, Peggy, your getting out and auditioning. That's very courageous of you. The baby's how old, Gladys?

GLADYS: Two months.

STUART: Two months. Good for you. Welcome back.

PEGGY: Thank you, Stuart. I told Gladys, how much fun it was just rehearsing with her.

DAVID: Really nice, Peggy.

STUART: When are you and Joe going to bring Miranda around so we can all fawn over her? My wife's been asking that, haven't you? We can't wait to fawn.

GLADYS: We should go and visit them, Stuart.

STUART: Let's find a time.

PEGGY: Whenever you're free. Come any time, I'm always there. I'm always free. *(To Joe)* Aren't I?

JOE: You're getting out.

STUART: Thank you, Peggy.

PEGGY *(To Joe)*: Should I go?

JOE: Peggy ordered us all a little lunch.

PEGGY: You did that. Just sandwiches.

JOE: It was Peggy's idea.

MERLE: What a nice idea.

GLADYS: Maybe it's here. Peggy, maybe we should go and check. See if it's here.

(Peggy starts to pick up her purse.)

Leave that. We're coming right back.

PEGGY: Just sandwiches and some sodas . . . *(To Joe)* I only have the sitter until three.

DAVID: Joe's showed us some baby pictures, Peggy . . .

PEGGY: Oh, I have lots more. In my purse . . . I carry a stack of pictures about this big . . .

(Peggy and Gladys go.)

MERLE: I've seen them. I'd like to see them again.

DAVID: Sandwiches and sodas that's really great.

MERLE: You could have let her finish, Stuart.

STUART: That's where we stopped before, Merle. *(To Joe)* How long have they been rehearsing? Never mind. You really needn't have done this. You should not have gotten her to do this.

JOE: I didn't 'get' her to do anything. She asked to audition. It's been a while. She was a little nervous. I thought she did great. She's a very good actress. We all know that. We've all seen that. And I agree she wasn't right for your *Shrew* last summer. I understood that.

STUART *(To Merle)*: I thought Mary Bennett read rather well. I've seen her onstage. And she's more my idea of Olivia. Young. Too young to be mourning. That's what I'm after. I want to cast her.

MERLE: Why are you saying this to me?

STUART *(To David)*: What did you think, David?

JOE: So you already had your mind made up?

STUART: I told you I wanted to cast this girl from Stratford. And you said, you have to see her first. Well, now you've seen her. And now I'm going to cast Mary Bennett.

JOE: I think you're prejudiced.

STUART: Against what? That makes no sense.

JOE: Because she's my wife.

STUART: What are you talking about? Peggy just isn't my idea of Olivia. Okay? Let's just leave it at that, can we? Come on.

JOE: She wasn't your idea of Kate—

STUART: And I told you that then. And I told her.

JOE: And she accepted that. I did too.

STUART: Anyway, isn't she now really too busy being a mom? She looks so great. She looks happy.

JOE: One big reason I started this theater, Stuart, was to give Peggy a place to act. I've told you that. She's a wonderful actress.

STUART: Actually you never have. Not like that. Is that true? I don't think it's true. I hope it's not true.

JOE: Haven't I told you that Merle?

MERLE: All the time.

STUART: Please don't make me hurt her.

JOE: I don't want her hurt.

STUART: What you're asking is unfair to me. To all of us. For god sake, is this a real theater or not?

(Looks at the others.)

You know they all agree with me . . . Merle?

MERLE: Leave me out of this, Stuart.

STUART: Okay, I'm glad we saw her. Maybe this helps her get back used to auditioning. I hope so. She did great. Happy to be of some help to Peggy, who is a friend. So—now let's cast Mary Bennett as our Olivia. All right?

JOE: I don't agree.

STUART: Then get another director.

MERLE: Stuart—

JOE: Then I will.

MERLE: Joe . . .

STUART: Really? Good. Good. Thank god. It's off my back.

JOE: Someone better.

MERLE: Stop it.

STUART: Good luck. I couldn't be happier.

MERLE: Stuart— Where's lunch, I think we're hungry?

JOE: Merle, you know what this is about?

STUART: This has nothing to do—

JOE: He's looking for any excuse— David, he thinks he doesn't need us anymore.

STUART *(Hundredth time)*: I can do both jobs—

JOE *(Over this)*: T. Edward Hambleton bought him off! Poached him like a goddamn whore and bought him off! You know there's a name for that kind of person.

STUART (*Trying to make a joke to Merle*): A name besides 'whore'?

(*Having heard the argument, Gladys and Peggy enter with the lunch.*)

PEGGY: We have pastrami. And turkey.
GLADYS: Peggy and Joe bought us sodas too.

(*They take out the food from the bags.*)

STUART: Thanks, Joe. Thanks, Peggy.
DAVID: Stuart was just telling us about his wonderful new job.
PEGGY: Sounds really great. You'll be great.
DAVID: We're all 'sucking up.'
STUART: Not everyone.

(*As food is set out:*)

DAVID: We're all now 'sucking up' to Stuart . . .
PEGGY: Stuart, I was just telling Gladys, I'm not sure I'm even right for the role. Actually, I, and Joe knows this . . .
JOE: What?
PEGGY: Half the time I wake up and think, should I really be doing this anymore?
GLADYS: Every actress friend I know wakes up like that once, twice a week.
JOE: That's what I tell her.
PEGGY: Anyway, I know you'll want to have choices. You always should have choices . . .
DAVID: Where are all those baby pictures, Peggy? May I see? Please.

(*She gets them out of her purse.*)

STUART (*To Merle*): I can do both the Phoenix and the festival. If that's what Joe wants.

PEGGY: Joe wants that. He needs you. The two of you have built this.

MERLE: Pastrami?

STUART *(Suddenly stands up)*: Excuse me, I've got work to do. We'll talk about this later.

MERLE: Stuart, come on. Stop it.

STUART: Peggy, please bring the baby around some time. I'd love to meet her. I'm sure she looks like you . . . *(Nods)* Merle.

MERLE: Stuart, calm down. And have your goddamn lunch.

GLADYS *(Over this)*: Please, eat your lunch.

DAVID *(To Stuart)*: Aren't we going to the movies?

STUART *(To David)*: I don't feel like a movie right now. Merle, since when did he start putting "Joseph Papp presents" all over every fucking thing? I'm the one who directs all the fucking shows.

(Stuart is gone.)

JOE: He couldn't even say that to my face.

MERLE: I thought he did. You were right here . . .

JOE: Directors are a dime a dozen in this town . . . Aren't they, Merle?

MERLE: I don't know. Are they?

JOE: He's an asshole. How long have we known that?

PEGGY: Joe . . . Gladys is his wife.

GLADYS: It's all right. *(To Joe)* Sometimes Stuart can be like that, I know.

JOE: The Phoenix—there's just a vanity theater. If a rich guy wants to throw his money away—no one criticizes that. Stuart's too 'grand' for us now, Peggy.

GLADYS: I don't think that's true.

JOE: He runs 'the Phoenix.' And I thought loyalty still counted for something. I'm so naive.

MERLE: He's just blowing off steam, Peggy.

PEGGY: Who?

MERLE: Full of himself. Doesn't want to listen to anything or anybody. *(To Joe)* Stuart.

PEGGY: Is this about me?

JOE: No. No.

PEGGY: I told you he didn't want me. He didn't want me for Kate.

JOE: That was Kate. This is not about you. I could direct the damn play, Merle . . .

MERLE: Stuart will direct. Joe, he's just—

JOE: Stuart's leaving because—

MERLE *(Over this)*: He's not leaving. He *also* has another job. Who doesn't do two jobs? You do two jobs.

(As they eat:)

DAVID: Yesterday, a guy from the *Village Voice*—he came and interviewed Stuart.

MERLE: What? I didn't know that.

JOE: I don't know about this.

DAVID: Stuart thought it'd be 'cool' to do the interview on the stage.

MERLE: Who was it, Michael Smith? I should know about things like that. I should be told—

JOE *(To Merle)*: Why didn't he tell you?

MERLE: They're supposed to ask me first.

DAVID: So I moved my stuff. And I sat in the wings, pretending to work out some charts. The things Stuart said. The man is so goddamn full of himself. Full of bullshit. And—he's my friend.

MERLE: Glad you added that. I was going to remind us all of that.

JOE: He said to me the other night—talk about full of himself—

GLADYS: You told me this.

JOE: —that he doesn't think we're really serious. About raising money. "If we want to be a serious theater, Joe . . ." He's all about money, Stuart.

MERLE: Nothing wrong with money.

JOE: "T. Edward Hambleton knows how to raise money." Sure, he knows how to write himself a goddamn check.

DAVID: They're paying real salaries, he said.

JOE *(Over this)*: I told him we were damn serious. I told him we were going to have a big benefit.

MERLE: Are we? *(To Peggy)* What benefit? Anyone else know about a benefit?

PEGGY: No.

JOE *(Over the end of this)*: I'll be setting up a benefit committee.

MERLE: When did he decide—?

JOE: I'm going to ask Scott. And set a goal for—let's round it at—at an even million.

MERLE: A million dollars, Joe?

PEGGY: You think that's realistic?

JOE: Merle, do you think we can do it?

MERLE: Why not?

DAVID *(Handing back the photos)*: She's so sweet . . .

(David hasn't eaten.)

JOE *(To David)*: You don't want a sandwich?

PEGGY *(To Joe)*: I should go soon.

MERLE: A million . . . Why the hell not?

JOE: And in the meantime, Merle and I have agreed—that this summer we'll pass a hat. Before and after each show. Like in a church.

DAVID: Or on the Bowery. Just joking.

PEGGY: I thought you weren't allowed to do that. In the park. No begging . . .

JOE: This isn't 'begging.' Anyway, aren't rules meant to be broken? And besides what are they going to do? Arrest us? It's a play . . .

MERLE: Kerr wrote some nice things about us today.

DAVID: More about Scott? He loves Scott.

MERLE: Yeah. Still the son of a bitch couldn't resist beating his drum again.

DAVID: Not again.

MERLE: We must 'charge something.' 'Doesn't have to be a lot, just fucking something . . .' He won't quit. We'll write him again, Joe.

DAVID: We can't charge. That's our union deal.

MERLE: Which I think is also a good thing.

JOE: So we'll pass the hat. Before *and* after . . .

MERLE: And then we'll have Joe's benefit.

JOE: It's not a joke.

PEGGY *(With the photos)*: Merle, I was with Miranda in Washington Square the other day?

MERLE: What? *(A joke)* Joe says you never got out.

PEGGY: By myself. I never go out by myself. I had Miranda. And that's fine . . . *(Continues)* And all these mothers with baby carriages and their kids—they were raising a ton of money.

DAVID: I know about this.

MERLE *(Over this)*: Money for what?

DAVID: A road the city wants to build through the middle of the park.

GLADYS: Washington Square?

DAVID: They're fighting that.

JOE: Good luck.

DAVID *(Over this)*: And raising money.

GLADYS: What about the fountain?

DAVID: I don't think it's going to happen, Gladys.

PEGGY: Their buckets were almost completely full.

MERLE: That's good.

DAVID: I think they're backing off, Gladys. The city.

MERLE: Or just waiting them out. Waiting out the mothers.

PEGGY: Maybe I should carry Miranda around in my arms when we pass the hat? Seems to work.

JOE: Good idea.

GLADYS: Like the Gypsies.

DAVID: Smudge a little dirt on her face.

GLADYS: And in her cute little bear outfit.

PEGGY: Merle bought her that.

JOE: And who knows, maybe they'll be so busy fighting off the mothers, that they'll just forget all about us. *('Calls out')* Go after the mothers!

PEGGY: I really need to go.

(She starts to pick up.)

JOE: I'll walk you out.

GLADYS: I should go, too. *(Getting up)* Do you mind if I work in your office, Joe? I should write some letters . . .

JOE: Take another sandwich.

GLADYS: I've had plenty. Joe, you know my husband sometimes says things that he doesn't mean. And later regrets. I can attest to that. But he loves our festival. He really does. But if he doesn't want to direct this play, and he will regret that, I'm sure, then I think you, Joe, *would* be a very good choice. I really do, Joe. You should really consider it. Please do. To hell with him. Pardon my language. That's what I think, for what it's worth. Thanks for lunch. Both of you. Bye, Peggy.

PEGGY: I'm going too. *(To Gladys)* And thanks for all the help rehearsing.

GLADYS: And you did great. Didn't she, guys?

MERLE: She did.

DAVID *(Same time)*: You really did . . .

GLADYS: Bye.

PEGGY: Bye.

(Gladys is gone.)

PEGGY: That woman is devoted to this theater . . .

MERLE: I know.

PEGGY: It can't be easy for her. Don't leave this for John.

MERLE: We'll pick up, Peggy.

PEGGY: We always leave it for John.

JOE *(Again)*: I'll walk you out.

PEGGY: You don't have to.

JOE: I want to. You've hardly eaten anything . . . Merle, just before Miranda was born? *(About Peggy)* She was—this big. *(Smiles)*

PEGGY: Joe . . .

JOE: Sometimes she let me come to class. She did this scene with Colleen—

PEGGY *(Smiles)*: Oh that.

JOE: —and my god she held her own.

MERLE: That's something. To hold your own with Colleen.

JOE: That's what I'm saying, Merle. From some Shaw play.

PEGGY: Stella was impressed.

MERLE: I should go too . . .

DAVID: Me too.

PEGGY: Good to see you, David.

DAVID: You too, Peggy.

PEGGY *(To Joe)*: I'm going to take the subway. I don't need to take a cab.

(They are gone.)

MERLE: Welcome back!

DAVID: Welcome back!

MERLE: You going downtown?

DAVID: Yeah.

MERLE: Me too. You want to go through the park and down the west side?

DAVID: Good idea. I've been stuck inside this theater all day.

(John appears.)

JOHN: What's Peggy doing here? I haven't seen her in ages.

MERLE: She's had a baby, John.

JOHN: I know that.

JOHN (*About the food*): What's all this?

MERLE: Have a sandwich and a soda.

DAVID: Compliments of Joe and Peggy Papp. It'll just go to waste.

JOHN (*Taking a sandwich*): Thanks . . . I haven't had lunch yet. Long day already.

DAVID: I'm sure. Sounds like it. Fucking George C. Scott . . .

JOHN: You know I never got him into a cab. When I took Mary to the subway, we saw him still sitting on a bench in the park.

DAVID: By the way, your Mary's something, John. She is really something. Lucky you.

JOHN: Oh I know. How'd her audition go? She didn't know. Do you know?

DAVID: No, I don't know.

MERLE: I don't know . . .

(*They go.*
Alone, John begins to eat his sandwich.
Lights fade.)

Scene 2

Sunday, June 22, 1958. Early afternoon.

Colleen's apartment on the Upper West Side, near the park. Tables put together for a lunch party; piano, chairs and a bench set around the tables; rugs; two large arm chairs; a side table. Street noise throughout the scene.

Peggy is setting tablecloths over the tables, and will set out the plates, etc. Merle sits. Joe and Bernie sit at the table and sing together; David plays the piano, sight-reading from sheet music.

JOE AND BERNIE *(Singing)*:

> . . . and giddy with care, busy counting your profit and
> losses,
> Showing the might of you name unto god—
> in the gay-colored page of a checkbook . . .

(They emphasize "checkbook."
Colleen and then Gladys will enter with a tray of glasses;
pitchers of iced tea and lemonade.)

> Storing the best of your life in a draw'r of your desk at
>   the office:
> Bellow goodbye to the buggerin' lot 'n' come out

(They emphasize "buggerin' lot.")

> To bow down the head 'n' bend down the knee to the
>   bee, the bird, 'n' the blossom . . .
> Bann'ring the breast of the earth with a wonderful
>   beauty . . .

(They finish.)

BERNIE: "Wonderful beauty . . ."
JOE: "Wonderful beauty." Amazing we still can remember this,
    Bernie.
BERNIE: "Bellow goodbye to the buggerin' lot."
GLADYS: Lunch is almost ready.
COLLEEN: I need to tune that. *(The piano)*

(Colleen will head back to kitchen.)

PEGGY: Would that have helped?

(Mary has come in with beers.)

MARY *(To Gladys)*: Where should I—?
GLADYS: Hand them out.

(Gladys heads off to the kitchen.)

DAVID *(The sheet music)*: What is this?

MERLE: Don't ask. Oh god, please don't ask.

BERNIE: From a play, David, that takes place inside a park.

MERLE *(To David)*: O'Casey.

JOE: From our youth. When we were kids. A park play, Bernie. I forgot that. And so it's like I've just gone full circle.

(Takes a beer.)

DAVID: What do you mean?

MARY *(To Joe)*: Do you need . . . ? *(A bottle opener)*

BERNIE *(Has a bottle opener on a key chain)*: I got it.

JOE: A park. I'm back in a park. Full circle . . .

(Gladys and then Colleen return with dishes for lunch.)

BERNIE: Maybe you should just change your name to the New York O'Casey Festival.

GLADYS: That'll help with fundraising.

BERNIE: Stick it to the rich.

GLADYS: That will help with fundraising.

MERLE: 'Give us money and we'll stick it to you.' It has its own ring.

JOE: We have been there, and we have done that.

MARY: Been where??

JOE: We were there with this. *(The O'Casey play)*

MERLE *(To Mary)*: They did an O'Casey.

DAVID: I didn't know them then.

BERNIE *(Over this to Joe)*: And you still owe me the two hundred bucks—

MARY: What two hundred—?

JOE *(Over this)*: Forget it, Bernie.

PEGGY *(Same time, to Mary)*: Don't ask.

MERLE *(Explaining to Mary)*: They produced some play—

GLADYS: Joe directed it.

PEGGY *(Explaining to Mary)*: An O'Casey . . .

MERLE: A million years ago.

BERNIE: We're not all that old, Merle. We're still kids!

PEGGY *(To Colleen)*: I can vouch for that.

COLLEEN: Me too.

BERNIE *(Back to the O'Casey story, to David)*: Joe directed it. My god! Where's my money?

JOE: It wasn't the directing, Bernie.

MERLE *(To Bernie)*: You'll never see that two hundred dollars.

DAVID: What's this?

BERNIE: He *(Joe)* said it was a loan. He signed a piece of paper.

(They have done this joke many times:)

JOE: That was a 'thank you note,' Bernie. *(To the others)* Thank you for the two hundred dollars. *He* wanted to invest in theater. *Bernie!* With his own money!

BERNIE *(Feigned shock)*: *That* was an investment?!

(They laugh.)

PEGGY: Is there another beer? One for me?

MARY: There are plenty of beers in Colleen's icebox . . .

(She heads back to the kitchen.)

David brought the beer . . . Colleen, what else?

COLLEEN *(To Mary)*: And the water pitcher next to the sink . . . *(Sees that the water pitcher is already out)* Never mind.

(Mary is gone.)

GLADYS: And there's lemonade . . . .

DAVID: I brought the beer. At least I did that.

PEGGY: I think we're ready for you, gentlemen.

GLADYS *(To Colleen)*: Does it matter where we sit?

COLLEEN: Joe at the head . . . Anywhere else . . .

JOE *(A great memory)*: O'Casey, Bernie.

GLADYS *(To Joe)*: You're there . . . *(The head of the table)*

COLLEEN: David, it's out of tune. I'm sorry.

DAVID: It's fine. I don't really play the piano . . .

BERNIE: I think they know that now.

(They slowly take their seats.)

GLADYS: Sit anywhere.

MERLE: You'll never see that money, Bernie.

BERNIE: I know. I know. You don't have to tell me.

COLLEEN: What are you talking about?

MERLE: His two hundred bucks.

BERNIE: I found the sheet music in a shoebox of old stuff.
I thought it'd be fun . . .

PEGGY: It is. *(To Joe)* It's fun to hear you guys sing.

MERLE: You were mostly in the kitchen.

PEGGY *(To Bernie)*: Sit by me.

COLLEEN: Maybe on purpose.

MERLE: That's what I thought.

BERNIE: It was in the back of my closet. I'd forgotten all about
it. *(A joke to Joe)* Some things it's best to forget . . . .

MERLE: Who made all this?

PEGGY: Gladys mostly.

GLADYS: That's not true.

PEGGY: It's true, Gladys. *(Starts a list)* Your macaroni salad—

GLADYS: That's all I know how to make.

(Mary comes out with more beers.)

PEGGY: That's not true.

GLADYS *(Pointing out a dish)*: Mary brought that . . .

MARY: What did I bring? Did I do something wrong?

COLLEEN: No . . . *(Smiles)*

GLADYS *(Over this)*: The meatballs.

DAVID *(To Mary)*: Why did you think you—?

PEGGY: They look delicious.

(She has picked up a beer.)

BERNIE: Let me open that . . .
MARY *(To Peggy)*: My mother's recipe.
PEGGY *(To Gladys)*: And that's yours. And that.
GLADYS: Okay. Okay.
PEGGY: I didn't make anything. Sorry.
GLADYS: You just got back.
DAVID *(To Mary)*: Here, you're sitting next to me.
MERLE: Do you always do what he tells you to?
MARY *(Smiling)*: Almost never.
DAVID: Mary brought the potato salad . . .
BERNIE: Your mother's recipe?
MARY: Not that. I didn't make that. I bought it.
COLLEEN: Don't tell them that. Pass this over . . .

(She hands a dish to pass; and other dishes are passed around.)

DAVID *(Over this)*: Looks so good . . . *(To Mary)* Especially the
    'homemade' potato salad . . .
MARY: It isn't homemade.
MERLE: He's teasing you.
MARY: I know.
COLLEEN *(Holding up a dish)*: Who didn't get—? Merle?
MERLE: I'm fine, Colleen.
GLADYS: You have a beer, Joe? What happened to Joe's beer?
MERLE: Give him a beer. He should have a beer.
BERNIE: He had one.
MERLE: Where did you leave it?
JOE: I left it over . . . [by the piano].
MERLE: I got it . . .

(Merle gets Joe his beer.)

COLLEEN: What time do you have to get back, Bernie?

BERNIE: I have time . . . Joe, I'm meeting Houseman in Grand Central. Before the train. Some bar. We're taking the train back together.

COLLEEN: God bless that man . . . The shit has started hitting the fan up there. Or so one hears.

PEGGY: In Stratford?

COLLEEN: That's what George says.

JOE *(To Bernie)*: So what's happening in Stratford? What sort of shit has been hitting the fan, Bernie?

(All are interested.)

BERNIE: Three, four board members . . .

JOE: 'Board members.' Hell with them.

BERNIE *(Sips his beer)*: Fuck 'em.

COLLEEN: George said he'd heard they want you out, Bernie. The board there. That's what he heard. I told Peggy this. George has friends up there . . . But Houseman is standing by you?

BERNIE: He's gotten some of the actors with him.

COLLEEN: Good. Good.

PEGGY: You'd expect that.

MERLE: Not necessarily.

BERNIE: Some . . . of the actors . . . I'm told to expect most of the *crew*—they may not choose to talk to me. Cold shoulder stuff. That kind of thing.

JOE: Not easy when you're the stage manager.

BERNIE: No. *(Smiles)* No.

DAVID *(To Bernie, a joke)*: So they won't be talking back . . . The crew.

BERNIE: That's always good. A nice change.

COLLEEN: Bernie, the crew's busy not speaking to you and the board's busy trying to hang you from a flagpole. Do they have time up there to do any theater? What the hell are you rehearsing?

BERNIE: *Midsummer* and *Hamlet*. I'm stage managing *Hamlet*.

COLLEEN *(To Mary)*: In Stratford.

MARY: I understood. I've worked in—

DAVID *(To others)*: Mary worked in Stratford.

GLADYS: We saw you.

MERLE: This is the Fritz Weaver *Hamlet*?

DAVID: Is that a good idea?

COLLEEN: Who else?

BERNIE: Geraldine as Gertrude. Morris . . . Ellis Rabb is the Player King.

COLLEEN: Oh god. Haven't we already seen that?

GLADYS: What do you mean?

COLLEEN: You go to a bar with Ellis and you'll see his Player King.

PEGGY: You go to the post office with Ellis—

PEGGY AND COLLEEN: '—and you'll see his Player King.'

COLLEEN *(Mimicking Ellis, to Joe)*: "Out, out thou strumpet Fortune!"

PEGGY: That's him buying a stamp!

BERNIE: It's a memorable Player King . . .

COLLEEN: One of those memories you can't ever get out of your head. No matter how hard you try. How hard you scrub. It's still in there . . . You just can't shake it out.

PEGGY: Like a jingle . . .

COLLEEN: Except louder.

JOE: Maybe we'll come up and see it.

BERNIE: I'd love that, Joe.

JOE: Now that I've got the time. *(Trying to make a joke)* Sounds like you'll need someone to talk to up there . . .

BERNIE: Ellis is saying most of the lines.

COLLEEN *(To Bernie)*: I wouldn't want to have to stage manage . . .

BERNIE *(Continues)*: Just not always the *same* lines.

    (To Joe) And I'm very sorry about you losing your job. That's so fucking wrong.

MERLE: They really should know better.

BERNIE: Since when should CBS know better? Anyway, fuck 'em. Joe Papp doesn't need their damn job.

JOE: I expected nothing less from them. I'd have been shocked had they done anything less.

BERNIE: Me too.

PEGGY *(To Joe)*: That's not what you've been saying.

GLADYS: Peggy just got back last night.

BERNIE: You must be very tired.

PEGGY: We were two hours late.

BERNIE *(To Joe)*: Did you pick them up?

GLADYS: Joe did.

JOE: What do I have to do? I have nothing to do . . .

BERNIE: Tired?

PEGGY: No, I'm really not. I'm not. It's good to be back. It was hard being away. Really really hard.

COLLEEN: I'll bet.

MARY: I can imagine.

GLADYS: She didn't want to go . . .

BERNIE *(To say something)*: Pan Am?

PEGGY: Yes. My mother's with the baby now. Probably both asleep. *(Smiles)*

COLLEEN: What?

PEGGY: I'm not sure Paris is the place to go with your mother.

COLLEEN: Not with my mother!

(They laugh.)

MARY: See any theater there? I've never been to Paris. I've never been anywhere.

PEGGY: I didn't, Mary. I don't really speak French.

BERNIE: It was probably good for you to be away . . .

PEGGY: I don't know.

JOE: I agree . . .

BERNIE: It wasn't fun.

PEGGY: That's what my parents thought. And Joe. I wanted to stay . . .

BERNIE: It was probably easier for Joe—

PEGGY *(To Joe)*: I'd have *happily* sat there with you, next to you—

JOE: I know, and held my hand— And yours too, Bernie—
I know. Peggy, we know. But your parents were right. One
less thing to think about. Worry about.

PEGGY: 'Thing'?? Come on, Joe.

JOE: You know what I mean. And it made your parents calm
down a bit—your not being here. They needed to calm
down . . .

GLADYS *(To Peggy)*: You must be tired.

PEGGY: I slept on the plane.

COLLEEN: I never can do that.

PEGGY: I didn't want to go.

JOE *(To 'Mary')*: Mary, her parents live in Utah.

MARY: I didn't know that.

JOE: So they *imagine* all sorts of things. Because there's nothing
out there to actually *see*? So you're always *imagining*.

BERNIE: What does that mean?

PEGGY: He likes Utah. At least, that's what you've told me.
Many times.

JOE: I do. I like Utah.

PEGGY *(To 'Colleen')*: I'm not sure I believe him now—

JOE: It was a joke.

PEGGY *(Again)*: I didn't want to go. And I think it was the hard-
est thing I've ever done in my life. Being away during all
this— I hated every minute I was away. Why I ever let my
parents talk me into going, I don't know . . .

BERNIE: For some reason I can't picture Joe Papp in the middle
of Utah. Of all places.

JOE *(Trying to make a joke)*: I don't know what the hell Peggy's
parents were 'imagining.' Knock down our door, grab my
wife and demand her to—what? Answer! Is your husband
a goddamn communist?!

(He laughs, no one else does.)

PEGGY: I would have said, you're not. I would have said anything.

(Then:)

COLLEEN: Peggy brought me back a lovely scarf.

PEGGY: They sell them in the street. They're really cheap.

COLLEEN *(To the women)*: I was telling her, we women should all go to Paris together sometime. Get a whole group together and just go over there.

MARY: I'd like to go. If I can afford it I'd really like to go. If I'm not doing a show—

MERLE: If you are not at Stratford.

COLLEEN *(Continuing)*: Just women.

MARY *(Trying to make a joke to David)*: Just women!

DAVID: Why do you say that to me?

COLLEEN: And have some fun. Gladys? What about you?

GLADYS *(To Peggy)*: What about the baby?

COLLEEN: Let the men do that for a change. I'd like to see Joe—

PEGGY: He does his share, Colleen. He does what he can. Miranda and I both missed him. We really did.

MARY: So when do we go to Paris? *(To David)* If the restaurant will let me out . . .

DAVID *(To Mary)*: I don't think they're serious . . .

MARY: You aren't serious?

COLLEEN: Joe, Peggy was saying in the kitchen that in Paris, she's pretty much learned all her lines.

BERNIE: For what—?

JOE: She's my Olivia.

BERNIE: Of course. I heard that. Congratulations.

PEGGY: We'll see.

GLADYS: She'll be great.

DAVID: Joe's directing.

BERNIE: I heard that too. Congratulations.

DAVID: Stuart got busy.

BERNIE: That's what I heard too.

DAVID: I'm doing the music.

MERLE: Who else?

COLLEEN: She was saying her mom helped her. When they were in Paris.

JOE *(Over this)*: She told me. That made me laugh.

COLLEEN: With her lines. I have this picture now in my head of the two of them sitting in a Paris café outside, smoking—

PEGGY: I don't smoke.

DAVID: Does your mom smoke?

PEGGY: No.

GLADYS: Her mom—this very handsome Mormon lady—

JOE: She is.

GLADYS: —reading Viola? That's very funny. I would have liked to have seen that.

JOE: Me too.

COLLEEN: She's going to be great . . .

GLADYS *(A joke)*: Her mom?

MARY *(To Peggy)*: I could help out too. Running lines. If your mother gets tired. Any time.

PEGGY: I may take you up on that, Mary. I just may. Watch out.

MARY: I mean it. I do.

DAVID: I know she does.

MARY: It helps me too. Just running lines. I like it.

BERNIE: When do you start?

JOE: In a few weeks. So I'll be busy for a while . . .

GLADYS: I've been reading a lot of books about *Twelfth Night*.

JOE: Good. That'll help . . . I need the help.

COLLEEN: George called me from the set this morning and when I told—about us getting together today . . . About it being your birthday, Joe— He wanted to make sure I passed along his happy birthday.

JOE: Thank you, George.

COLLEEN: He's still filming.

PEGGY *(To Merle)*: It's his first movie. Colleen told me. I hadn't realized it was his first.

MERLE: I hadn't either . . . Good for him.

MARY: Colleen, is George coming back into your play? I loved the play. Did I tell you that?

COLLEEN: You told me. I really loved doing it. Two more weeks.
We're going to close. *(To Mary)* Thank you.

MARY: And you were really great.

MERLE: A good run. For this season a good run.

COLLEEN: A good run. *(Smiles, others laugh)* Very good!

PEGGY: Especially for you!

(The women laugh.)

COLLEEN: Especially for me!

GLADYS *(Over this)*: For her.

MARY: Why?

PEGGY: She met George!

GLADYS *(Same time)*: George!

MARY: Of course. George!

(They laugh.)

DAVID: Colleen, I just hope you're still laughing . . .

(The men laugh.)

GLADYS: What do you mean?

DAVID: He is—George . . .

MERLE: George . . .

COLLEEN: He's better now. A lot calmer. Must be me. *(To the women)* George Scott is who he is. You accept that and the rest is easy.

PEGGY *(Pushing forward)*: He is going to do a play . . .

MERLE: When? I haven't heard—?

PEGGY: Colleen told me.

COLLEEN: In the fall. And it's going to tour. Then come in. George is so upset about—for both of you. *(Turns to Joe)* And Joe, he asked if you'd ever consider—doing him a favor, and stage managing this play. He's sure he could arrange that. He says he's pretty sure they haven't hired anyone yet.

PEGGY *(Knows the answer, to Colleen)*: In the fall?

JOE *(Eating)*: Did George suggest this or did you call him back and ask? Or beg?

PEGGY: Joe, it's a job. You need a job.

COLLEEN: Joe, George wasn't—

MERLE: They'd be so lucky to have you as their stage manager—

JOE: I'm not just a goddamn stage manager, Merle. I'm not.

PEGGY *(To Colleen)*: We'll talk about it . . .

JOE: About what?

PEGGY: I think it would just be an easy thing to do. To fill this time. You've got some time, as you just said. Thank you, Colleen. And thank George. We will sleep on it.

BERNIE *(To Joe)*: Did you like your lawyer? We haven't even had the chance to compare notes . . .

JOE: We haven't seen each other.

MERLE: He had Ephraim. I got Ephraim for Joe.

BERNIE: I know. That's why I'm asking. You hear different things.

MERLE: About Ephraim?

JOE: I liked him.

MERLE: What do you hear?

PEGGY *(To Joe)*: You said he was very helpful.

JOE: Once, I was about to say . . .

(They listen, interested.)

I don't know what—to those sons of bitches. I felt his hand, his fingers on my elbow, digging in. *(Smiles)* 'Don't do it, Joe.' 'Don't do it.' Don't give them anything. Don't make them mad. Don't wave anything red in front of their faces . . .

BERNIE *(Answering Merle's question)*: That Ephraim can be a bit 'stiff.' That's all. *(To Joe)* I had Faulkner.

MERLE: Stanley.

DAVID *(Trying to make a joke, to Merle)*: Do you know all the lawyers? Why does Merle know all the lawyers?

COLLEEN: Merle knows everyone, and can fix everything. Everyone knows that.

MERLE: I wish. If only that were true, Colleen. God knows I try.

BERNIE *(To Joe)*: I wanted to give a statement. Faulkner didn't want me to.

PEGGY: Neither did Ephraim. *(To Joe)* Right? *(To the others)* Say as little as possible, and just get out of there. *(To Joe)* Isn't that right? That's what you told me.

JOE *(To Bernie)*: You were first. Before me . . .

COLLEEN: Were you, Bernie? I didn't know that.

MERLE: Bernie was on Wednesday.

BERNIE *(Continues)*: So the Committee was still 'fresh.' I kept saying but I don't even work in television or movies. I work in the goddamn theater. I thought this time around you're investigating just television and movies. So I said—the guy you really want to talk to is a guy named 'Joseph Papp.'

DAVID *(Serious)*: Bernie, you didn't—

MERLE: He's joking, David.

BERNIE: He works for CBS. He's in television. Did you catch that? 'Joseph Papp.' I slowed down so they could write it. 'I think he's coming in tomorrow. Talk to him.' I kept saying—can we hurry this up? I've got a matinee!

(He smiles.)

DAVID: I'm sure that went over well.

MERLE *(To David)*: He didn't really say it.

DAVID: I know.

BERNIE: I thought Arens looked like a fucking monkey.

JOE: Moulder was the really scary one, I thought. I keep thinking I'd cast him as one of the killers in *Macbeth*.

BERNIE: Angelo. In *Measure*.

JOE: Maybe. That fits too.

BERNIE: Houseman says it's not going to be an easy fight. With the board. They really want me out . . . And hanging from a tree. Or flagpole . . .

(Doorbell.)

DAVID: Who's that?

(Colleen goes to get the door.)

COLLEEN: I don't know . . .
MERLE: He came, Joe.
PEGGY: Who?
GLADYS: Who?

(Colleen returns with Stuart.)

COLLEEN: Look who the cat dragged in.
STUART: Sorry I'm late. What did I miss?
MERLE: You're late, Stuart.
DAVID *(Same time)*: Stuart! *(To Merle)* I thought he wasn't coming.
BERNIE: 'Mr. Broadway.'
STUART *(Over this)*: Good to see you too, Bernie. What the hell are you doing here? I heard they haven't fired you yet. And there are worse names to be called, thank you.
GLADYS: I thought you couldn't come.

(Stuart kisses Gladys.)

MERLE: Hi, Stuart. Glad you could fit us in. You're a busy man.
STUART: I *was* busy, Merle. Some of us do real work for a living.
MERLE: I work.
COLLEEN *(Over this)*: There's plenty of food.
PEGGY: I'll get him a plate, Colleen.
COLLEEN *(Following, to Mary)*: There's another chair in the kitchen. It's broken . . . *(Calls back)* Someone get him a beer.
MERLE: I got it . . . *(The beer)*

*(Colleen and Peggy go off.
Stuart is looking at Mary.)*

MARY *(Reminding him)*: Mary . . .

STUART: I know who you are. Why are you here? Is Robertson here?

MARY: No, no, he's not.

DAVID: Mary came with me . . .

STUART *(Penny drops)*: Oh. Ah. Well, good to see you. And you too, David. *(To Mary)* I hope Stratford hasn't stolen you away again.

MARY: No, no it hasn't. Not yet.

STUART *(To David)*: You are something.

DAVID: What do you mean? What does he mean? Who knows what he means?

(Laughter.)

MARY: Why are they laughing?

STUART: Nice to see you, Bernie. I mean it. It's been ages. I hear you have your hands full up there babysitting Ellis.

BERNIE: He's doing fine. They love him 'up there.' The suburbs.

JOE *(Greetings Stuart)*: Stuart . . .

STUART: Joe . . . .

BERNIE: I have to go soon.

STUART: I just got here.

MERLE: Maybe that's why.

BERNIE: Actually it is.

GLADYS *(Explaining)*: He's meeting up with Houseman.

(Colleen has returned with a chair. Peggy follows with a place setting.)

STUART: Where?

GLADYS: Bernie's taking the train back with him. He's trying to save Bernie's job.

STUART: From what I hear—good luck.

BERNIE: Thank you, Stuart, thank you. I so appreciate the concern. And the confidence.

STUART: I meant . . . I mean—good luck. Really.

MERLE: We know what you mean.

BERNIE *(To Stuart)*: Thanks. Hopefully I won't need 'luck.'

PEGGY *(Wiping her hands)*: Stuart, thank you for coming.

STUART *(Greeting)*: Peggy . . .

(They hug.)

PEGGY: Thank you. And isn't it good to see Bernie?

COLLEEN: We don't see him enough.

PEGGY: I know it means a lot to Joe.

STUART: I'm sure it does.

BERNIE *(Shrugs)*: It's his *(Joe's)* birthday . . .

PEGGY: Not just that.

COLLEEN *(Calls)*: Everyone come back to the table.

STUART: Joe's birthday? I didn't know that.

GLADYS: You didn't know it was his—?

STUART: No one told me. Why didn't you tell me?

COLLEEN: Come and sit down.

STUART *(Heading to the table)*: So that's what that was about. When he called this morning he made such a big point: 'Are you coming today?' 'Please, can you be here? It's important.'

COLLEEN *(To Stuart)*: You're there.

STUART: Do I have to sit next to Bernie? Why didn't you just say it was your birthday? *(A joke)* I'd still have come.

COLLEEN: The chair's a little broken . . .

STUART: Happy birthday. And I really meant to get here earlier.

(They all toast.)

EVERYONE: Happy birthday . . . Happy birthday . . .

STUART: I'm sorry. I didn't know . . .

(As they sit:)

DAVID: We hadn't toasted Joe yet.

STUART *(To Merle)*: How old? I'm sure he won't tell me.

MERLE: Twenty-five . . . In his heart.

PEGGY: Sometimes, I think—twelve. Even ten.

(Laughter.)

STUART *(To everyone)*: Really nice to be here. But I'm glad you didn't wait.

GLADYS: If we'd known you were coming . . .

MERLE: Would that have made a difference?

DAVID: I don't think so.

PEGGY: No.

COLLEEN: Not to me.

(Laughter.)

I don't know when I've had so many people in my apartment . . . Stuart, don't lean back in that *(Chair)*, it's broken. George leaned back, he broke it.

DAVID: Mary made the meatballs.

MARY: Stop it.

STUART: You *didn't* make them?

MARY: I did.

STUART: I don't understand.

MERLE: David keeps teasing Mary.

MARY: I don't care.

STUART *(To Mary, about David)*: Be careful of him.

GLADYS: Stuart.

STUART: I'm joking.

MERLE *(To Mary)*: He's not. Be careful of him.

MARY *(Smiling)*: I am.

(Laughter.)

STUART *(To Bernie)*: I really mean it—good luck.

JOE *(Getting their attention)*: Sh-sh. Sh-sh. Bernie has to leave soon. I'd like him to hear this.

STUART: What is this? His birthday speech?

MERLE *(To Stuart)*: You have enough to eat?

BERNIE *(To Stuart)*: I don't know.

GLADYS: I don't know either.

STUART *(To Merle)*: I have plenty.

JOE: Does everyone have what they need? David, you going to need another beer?

DAVID: I'm okay.

JOE: Yeah. My birthday speech.

MERLE *(To David, about the beer)*: You've finished that. I'll get it.

DAVID: I'm okay.

(Merle gets David another beer.)

STUART: Why are you so serious? He looks so serious.

JOE: I'm surprised, Merle, you could go this long without saying anything.

MERLE: You told me not to, Joe.

JOE: Since when did you do what I say?

(The room is curious now.)

PEGGY: What is this?

DAVID: Peggy, you don't know?

PEGGY: No.

JOE: Bernie needs to go fight for his job.

BERNIE *(Curious)*: I've got a little time.

JOE: Merle? You want to begin?

(Merle doesn't respond.)

Merle and I met this morning with Moses' people. Mostly his deputy, some asshole in the Parks Department—what was he, British?

MERLE: I don't know. Maybe. Really affected. The accent. The clothes. Everything.

JOE: 'Constable.' Right? His name.

DAVID *(To Merle)*: Why were you meeting—?

JOE: They asked. They summoned us.

DAVID *(To Merle)*: Where was this?

MERLE: The Arsenal.

PEGGY: This morning? You said nothing about this to me.

JOE *(Over the end of this)*: They wanted us to know they'd had a meeting with our unions.

STUART: What?? Who—?

MERLE: The parks people, Stuart. With our unions. Stage-hands. Actors . . . Teamsters . . .

PEGGY: I'm an actor.

MERLE: They all had a meeting together. And they didn't invite Joe. Didn't tell him about it. About a week ago. Did you know, Stuart?

STUART: No. Of course not. Why would I . . . ?

MERLE *(To Joe)*: I told you he didn't know.

JOE: This Constable, he has a ridiculous moustache. And acts like he's running India under the Raj. He'd be good casting for that. *(Salutes stiffly)* Didn't you think so, Merle?

MERLE: All he needs is the riding whip . . .

STUART: What about the unions? What was this meeting for . . . ?

(Joe has finished his beer.)

MERLE: You want another beer?

JOE: I got it, Merle . . . *(Gets up to get a beer from the side table)* Constable read a 'summary' someone had written—

MERLE: He wrote it. We're sure he wrote it himself.

JOE: —of this 'meeting' back to us. Everyone had been told not to tell us about this meeting. And, according to Constable's 'summary,' they spent the whole meeting just complaining about us. How poorly we pay people. How we 'use' people. Take advantage. And how everyone, all our unions, insist that we begin to charge money.

PEGGY: I thought we couldn't because we were in the parks. I thought there was a rule about that, in the parks.

MERLE: There was. Is. When we were downtown. That park. We guess they've just changed the rule . . . And so now they want us to charge. But we do that and our union deals have to change, Bernie.

BERNIE: Sure.

MERLE: So everything will cost more. But what the parks people are really hoping for, what we think this is really about—

DAVID: What?

MERLE: —is that by making us charge, fewer and fewer people will then come to see our shows, David. And the smaller the audiences, the harder for us to then raise money. While at the same time, now that we're charging, because of new union deals, we'll need to raise even more. And on and on, until in no time, a couple of years at most, we'll have just faded away . . .

DAVID: The festival?

MERLE: Joe tried to disagree . . . Tried to explain, we have deals with our unions; of course unions want more money, but we're 'free.' And when he did, Mr. Constable—he asked Joe, if this 'free' idea, was this a 'communist' thing, Mr. Papp?

PEGGY: He said that? What right does he have to say that?

MERLE: He said that almost in passing. Almost dismissive. At first I didn't know if I'd heard right. We didn't know what to say. Constable, he just stares at us. Then some assistant comes in, didn't even knock—

JOE: We think he was summoned. A buzzer under the desk?

MERLE: And reports to Constable that 'the mothers are furious with them this morning.'

GLADYS: What mothers? I don't understand.

MERLE: Constable doesn't wait for us to even ask. He wants to explain that in the middle of last night, just off Central Park West, they brought in bulldozers and buried a kids' playground, quickly poured the concrete and created fourteen spanking new parking spots for the fancy restaurant there. And now, Constable is grinning at us. 'Oh,' he says, 'the mothers are so furious with us.'

STUART: This to intimidate you.

MERLE: Show us what they can do if they want to. He then leans across his big fat desk and asks Joe, 'Mr. Papp, what kind of person takes the Fifth?'

DAVID: We're a goddamn Shakespeare festival . . .

COLLEEN: What do they want?

JOE: Their park? Because it's their park? Maybe to them we've been pissing in their park . . .

BERNIE: 'What kind of person takes the Fifth . . .'

MERLE: We know where that's headed. Right, Bernie?

BERNIE: Yeah . . .

PEGGY: He said that to you?

MERLE: After all what's happened this week. Even preparing these past weeks for the Committee, it has taken its toll. Joe told me . . . I can tell them, can't I? That he sometimes now, often, wakes up in the night, sweating and scared. He has a family.

DAVID: We can fight them, Joe.

JOE: I want to fight back, David. All things being equal, I'd fight. But . . . We know where that would likely end.

BERNIE: We do.

DAVID: Is the festival closing? Is that what you're saying?

JOE: This doesn't belong just to me, David. This is not a one-person vanity theater.

DAVID: Of course not.

GLADYS: What do you mean?

JOE: That's what you've always said, haven't you, Stuart?

STUART: I have.

JOE: So given everything, Merle and I have agreed, that the best thing is for me to back off now.

PEGGY: What does that mean?

JOE: To back off. Stuart, we're handing our festival over to you.

BERNIE: Shit . . .

GLADYS: Joe . . .

DAVID: For how long?

MERLE: We buy time. To raise money? Do some shows? For as long as it takes, David.

JOE: You take charge, Stuart. You decide everything. You be the boss. You're in a good position now. You've even got a rich guy behind you. And you're you and not me. Be our white knight. You're good casting for that. *(Smiles)* That's it. I'm done. Now who the hell has the bottle opener?

BERNIE *(Handing him his opener)*: Joe . . .

DAVID: This is so unfair.

JOE *(To Peggy)*: I'm fine . . . Stuart, say something. He's tongue-tied. I never saw you tongue-tied . . .

MERLE: Everyone, we're still hoping to do the two shows this summer.

GLADYS: Good.

JOE: Merle has written the press release. You should read it over. So—say something.

(No response.)

Nothing. That is a first.

MERLE: Some of our patrons will probably want Joe to keep a connection here. To the festival. And I'm sure we all want that too. At least for a while. *(To Joe)* A good while.

DAVID: Of course.

COLLEEN: Absolutely.

JOE: We'll keep that quiet.

MERLE: After all, this has been Joe's baby. He needs to remain a part of this in some way. As say a 'friend of the court'? I insisted on this. And Joe's agreed. That took some convincing. Here's the press release, Stuart.

(He sets the press release in front of Stuart.)

JOE: We all know what a wonderful director Stuart is . . .

DAVID: We do.

COLLEEN: You are.

JOE: And a good friend. You and I have paid our dues—in the trenches together.

STUART: We have, Joe.

MERLE: Here it is, Stuart. I can change anything.

JOE: A steady hand . . . To keep them at bay. It won't be easy. *('Smiles')* We'll be in good hands. *(About Gladys)* And this woman here, I highly recommend as an assistant. You could do far far worse . . . *(Smiles)* But you know that. As her husband . . .

(Stuart nods.)

(To Peggy) You okay?

PEGGY: I'm fine. I'm worried about you.

(He has taken the press release, then:)

STUART *(Quietly)*: I don't want it.

MERLE: What, Stuart? What did you say?

STUART: I said I don't want it, Merle.

JOE: What do you mean? I don't think I understand. You can do it and the Phoenix . . . We've assumed that, haven't we?

MERLE: We have.

DAVID: Stuart?

STUART: I don't want it. I love you. I love all of you. You're my friends. I gave you good advice. How many times have I told you—Joe, you run this 'festival' like it's all about Joe Papp? Now do you believe me?

JOE: I think this proves you are wrong, doesn't it?

MERLE: It does, Stuart.

COLLEEN: This is very generous of Joe.

STUART: I'll be the first to admit that our 'festival' has been great for me. And I am thankful for that. In the way, say like you step on a rock to cross a creek, to get to the other side. To get somewhere. Isn't that what this is? A way to get somewhere? David, you understand.

65

DAVID: Understand what?

STUART: Come on. And now—I am somewhere else.

GLADYS: Stuart.

STUART: I have another job. And Joe, everyone in this room knows that the festival is broke. Merle? Gladys? David? Colleen? Peggy? We're broke. We're broke, Bernie. Yet he *(Joe)* acts like— And not because of Robert Moses, Joe, for god's sake. Or his—'Constable.' Or the Parks Department.

JOE: Merle, I told you . . .

STUART: Told Merle what? That I wouldn't want it? Then why are you acting so surprised. I just want to be honest with all of you. I'd think you'd want that. I'd want that. Look, Joe makes it like he's giving me some great gift. What is he really trying to give me? Or is it: trying to pass off?

MERLE: That's not fair.

STUART *(Over this)*: Aren't you just trying to use me again?

JOE: 'Again'?

STUART *(Over this)*: As the one grown-up in the room. To save you from yourselves.

GLADYS: He's offering you the festival.

STUART: For Christ sake, you all pretend or maybe even believe that this 'festival'— What festival, Gladys? This summer, one week of *Othello* that we set up to do with George Scott—

COLLEEN: He got a movie—

STUART: I'm not blaming George, Colleen. Far from it. And then your and Peggy's—*Twelfth Night*, Joe. If you get that on. I hope you do . . . I'll be there to cheer you on, if you do. I will. Merle, I happen to agree with the unions. I don't think they were misrepresented as you implied. What's in it for them? That's exactly what they should be asking, isn't it? That's why there are unions. And now I'm simply asking, what we all should be asking: what's in it for me now? For any of us? Actually, maybe they've just done us all a real service, the Parks Department.

DAVID: What are you talking about?

STUART: By forcing us to now face the truth, David. And I'm now wondering, Joe, because you're a smart man, a very smart man, that maybe you've just realized too and now are simply trying to untangle yourself without saying so. And so dump this on me.

MERLE: He's not *dumping* anything—

DAVID *(Over this)*: Come on, Stuart.

GLADYS: I think you've said enough.

STUART *(Over this)*: I really hate being the only grown-up here. But I have accepted that responsibility for a while now.

(David gets up and moves away from the table.)

David, don't just walk away. See, that's what I mean. Why can't we be grown-ups? Isn't it time we heard the truth? Bernie, people come and sit on the grass or in chairs on a nice summer night in the park. And we think they are there only because of us? Because they so admire us?

BERNIE: I think so.

STUART: Gladys, you've heard me say the same a hundred times.

GLADYS: Say what, Stuart?

STUART: I think this Constable has simply told us what in our hearts we know is true. That the real reason we don't want to charge—

GLADYS: This is not true.

STUART: —is because we're afraid no one will come if we do.

DAVID: I don't think that.

GLADYS *(Same time)*: It's not true.

STUART *(Over this)*: So 'free,' it's just a way of avoiding failure. While at the same time it lets us pretend that we are above all that—what? Other stuff? Stuff that I'm now 'not above'? *(To Bernie)* "Mr. Broadway."

BERNIE: That was a joke.

STUART: I know. We in this room created this 'festival'—for one simple reason, to get our work seen, so we could move on. I'm moving on. Where's George Scott right now?

COLLEEN *(Again)*: He got a movie, Stuart.

STUART *(Over this)*: We decided to do *Othello* because of George Scott. Then George Scott gets a movie, and all of us are like—congratulations, lucky him, I wish it were me. I want to make movies too. This is what we want. We're ambitious. And that is a good thing, isn't it? To be ambitious? You tell me if someone came to you right now, David, and said—

DAVID: Stuart, please don't—

STUART: 'I want you to write music for these five shows at the Phoenix,' you'd say, 'Oh, but I have committed that time to these free plays in Central Park?' Well I've asked him, and he's said yes. *(To David)* Haven't you?

(No response from David.)

Merle, I think our press rep is tired, they need a change. I've told them about you. Peggy, if you want to audition . . . I can't promise anything, but . . . And—Robertson is going to stage manage for me. A whole season. And what's wrong with that? We're not kids anymore, 'making our own breaks.' You're right we have families. You have a child. Let's all now be grown-ups. That's what I've wanted to say to all of you, for a very long time . . .

GLADYS: Stuart, they are asking for your help.

STUART: And that is exactly what I'm trying to give, Gladys.

(Gladys starts to cry.)

I'm sorry. And this isn't easy for me, either. Gladys, maybe there is something I can do to help Joe.

GLADYS: Please, stop.

MERLE: Enough, Stuart. You've said more than enough.

STUART: No, let me help, Joe. We all need help. We all help each other. Joe, I've been offered this show in the fall. Broadway. Something I'm fitting in around the Phoenix.

Maybe you could be our stage manager. Robertson isn't free. He's busy at the Phoenix. We'd be so damn lucky to get you. What do you say?

GLADYS: Joe's not a stage manager, Stuart . . . And you're an asshole.

STUART *(Hurt)*: I'm an asshole? Why do you say that, Gladys? Have you heard a word I've said?

BERNIE: Stuart, what are you doing? These are your friends.

STUART: I know that, Bernie. I know—that's what I've been trying to say. Come on, what he's asking of me—isn't fair. It really isn't. And I think he knows it. Gladys, what a terrible thing to say. In front of our friends.

(Pause.)

Fuck. I better go. I'm not really hungry . . .

BERNIE: Stuart . . .

STUART *(As he goes)*: Happy birthday . . .

(He is gone.
Silence.
Joe stands.)

JOE: Excuse me.

DAVID: Fuck him.

PEGGY: Joe, what are you doing?

MERLE: Joe, what good is—?

BERNIE: Don't fight him. Damn it. That won't help.

(Joe goes.)

MERLE *(Standing, to Bernie)*: Should I go—

GLADYS *(To Merle)*: Joe won't catch him. We know my husband.

BERNIE: And even if Joe does— Joe's not a puncher, he's a chest thumper. They'll just bruise each other . . .

DAVID: I'm sitting here listening and thinking—do I just go over there, reach down and rip out his balls? 'Grow up'??

(Short pause.)

COLLEEN *(To Gladys)*: Do we think we're done? Are we done? Maybe we should take some of this into the kitchen . . . Mary?

MARY: I'll help . . .

DAVID: We're grown-ups.

BERNIE *(To David)*: You're doing five shows for Stuart?

DAVID: I can do both.

COLLEEN: I think we're done . . .

(Colleen and Mary start to pick up some dishes, plates, etc.)

DAVID: So what now? Is that it? Fuck him.

BERNIE: Merle, is there nothing else you can do? Why do they really care? So you piss in their park. Haven't they got other things more important? It doesn't make sense.

MERLE: There's more.

BERNIE: What do you mean?

MERLE: Like Joe said. We got sandbagged. They called us in. They didn't say anything about any meeting with the unions. And we still don't know what was really said. We assumed we were there to explain our request, why we needed to raise money by asking people at the shows—you know, give something. Pass the hat . . . Why we should be allowed to do this even though it's against park rules. 'No—begging.' Constable banged on the desk: 'No *more* begging.' Maybe it was the banging, but Joe then got a little full of himself— *(Smiling)* You probably haven't noticed but Joe Papp can sometimes get a little full of himself . . .

DAVID: Really?

BERNIE *(Joking)*: Oh I've never seen that . . .

MERLE: He's telling Constable—sir, you don't understand what a park is for. *(Incredulous)* We're in the headquarters of the Parks Department . . . *(Continues)* 'A park needs people,' he explains to the head deputy of the Parks Department.

(Smiles) 'And in *their* own park, people shouldn't have to pay . . .' I'd given him that line. Then Constable just interrupts and tells us about this meeting with the unions. How, he said, we are seen by them. Once again how *beggars* aren't allowed in the parks. 'For everyone's protection.' How this will now be strictly enforced. And about the new so-called Lincoln Center.

DAVID: What . . . ?

BERNIE *(Same time)*: What about the Lincoln Center?

MERLE: How there's going to be a park there too in the fucking Lincoln Center.

DAVID: I didn't know that.

BERNIE: Me neither.

MERLE: And how they—and who the hell is 'they' I don't know—rich people, I guess—how they are thinking of doing their own fucking outdoor summer Shakespeare festival. In this 'park.' So once theirs is built, in a couple of years, 'Why the hell will we need two?'

PEGGY: That's just stealing from us.

MERLE: See it's not that they don't want Shakespeare—in a park. It's that they want their own fucking Shakespeare in their own fucking park. Their fucking rich person's park. So they can fucking run it. Own it. Decide who can and can't get into it. And, to control that, charge whatever the fuck they want . . .

(Joe enters.)

So what happened?

JOE: He ran down the stairs . . . The elevator button had been pushed. He must have heard me coming and ran down the stairs.

MERLE: Why didn't you take the elevator and beat him down the stairs?

(Joe looks at him.)

You probably wouldn't have beaten him. If he was running . . . .

DAVID *(To Joe)*: Are you okay?

JOE: We're going to do *Twelfth Night* even if it kills us. I'll show that son of a bitch. I just decided that.

BERNIE: Good.

JOE *(To Peggy)*: And you'll be a wonderful Olivia. You were born to play that part.

COLLEEN: That's right. You were.

PEGGY: I don't need to play Olivia.

JOE *(To Merle)*: But we're going to have to change something now, Merle. No more—'free.' To get them off our backs.

MERLE *(Over this)*: It's not about that. They just want us out. That's their excuse—

JOE: They win that.

COLLEEN: It's not their fucking park.

MERLE: Tell the mothers that as they bring their kids to the playground that's now a goddamn restaurant parking lot . . .

(Colleen, Mary and now Gladys will take dishes off to the kitchen.)

JOE: Bernie, fifty cents. For half of the seats. I've told Merle, what's the big deal? If that gets them off our backs for a while.

MERLE: It won't get Moses off our backs, Joe.

JOE: Just get off your high horse, Merle!

PEGGY: Joe, he's your friend.

MERLE: What 'high horse'?

JOE: Bernie, we haven't raised half, a third of what we need for the summer.

BERNIE: Why are you two talking to me?

JOE: They smell blood. After the Committee, CBS—everything said to denigrate—it hasn't exactly helped with fundraising.

MERLE: No.

JOE: So we have to charge something.

MERLE: We're on the same side, Joe. Why do I have to remind you of that?

JOE *(Continues to 'Bernie')*: And so if we have to charge a little . . . I don't think that's some 'climb down.' What great heights are we climbing down from?! We're just trying now to survive. *(To Merle) That* high horse, Merle.

(Colleen, Mary and Gladys have returned; they continue to take things off.)

COLLEEN: We're all on the same side here. Aren't we?

PEGGY: We are. We are.

BERNIE *(To lighten the mood)*: Mary, I once asked Joe, why do only Shakespeare plays in the park? You know what he told me? 'Because you don't have to pay royalties . . .' *(Smiles)*

MARY: Is that true?

BERNIE: That sounds like Joe. Doesn't it, Merle?

PEGGY: That sounds like him.

DAVID *(To Joe)*: I'm sorry. I was going to tell you. About the Phoenix shows.

JOE: It's okay.

MERLE: Joe, show Bernie your 'birthday card.' He insists on calling it his 'birthday card.' You said you were going to bring it . . .

(Joe takes a letter out of his pocket.)

JOE: I brought it. To show you, Bernie. I wanted to see your face . . . You will appreciate this.

GLADYS: Hear this.

JOE: They've all seen it.

(Hands the letter to Bernie.)

GLADYS: He wrote Stratford—

JOE *(To Bernie who has looked up from the letter)*: *Canada.* Stratford, Canada. Not Connecticut.

GLADYS: And said—we're struggling here. And we're a sister festival. And we're doing *Twelfth Night.*

JOE: And that I know you in Canada did a 'wonderful' *Twelfth Night*—I actually heard it was crap—'wonderful' *Twelfth Night* last season up there in Canada, so we're wondering could we please please—borrow your costumes? Because that would save us a lot of money this summer. Theater to theater? Shakespeare festival to Shakespeare festival?

BERNIE: And so what did they say?

JOE: Read it, Bernie. *(To the others)* From Michael Langham himself. Just read that . . . Out loud. Word for word. *(Points)* There . . .

BERNIE *(Reads)*: "I cannot, I'm afraid, agree with your policy over these matters. I think it is harmful to the profession to proclaim to audiences that our work is not worth paying for."

COLLEEN: Fucking Canadians.

MERLE: Langham's English.

COLLEEN: Fucking Brits. If I hear one more Brit tell me how to do Shakespeare—'Oh, dearie, you need to learn to breathe.' I fucking know how to breathe. I'm a human being! George does a very funny Brit. He prances around—

MERLE *(Laughing)*: I've seen him do that.

DAVID: I have too . . .

BERNIE *(Handing back the letter)*: So—no costumes . . .

Colleen, is there any whiskey? I'd like a whiskey . . .

DAVID: That sounds like a very good idea, Bernie.

JOE *(Over this)*: Colleen always has whiskey.

COLLEEN: What about the coffee?

GLADYS: Who wants coffee? *(To Colleen)* No one wants coffee.

COLLEEN: Mary, now we need glasses for whiskey.

(Mary gets up.)

MERLE: I'll have a whiskey . . .

GLADYS: No coffees? Peggy?

PEGGY: I'll have coffee.

(Colleen and Gladys, after picking up the last few things, head back into the kitchen. They will soon return.)

JOE *(To Merle)*: Fifty cents is not much. Who can't afford fifty cents? They'll still come.

MERLE: And next summer it will a buck, then the next and the next—

JOE: That's how we'll win.

MERLE: Win what? What will we have won?

BERNIE: Langham's a jerk. We all know that. And all you wanted was a free rental. Joe keeps trying the same thing with Connecticut Stratford. 'Sister festival.' They don't even answer him anymore there.

MERLE: Joe, I will do anything in my power, you know this, for free Shakespeare.

JOE: I know that, Merle.

MERLE: But, Joe, I'm not going to work for cheap Shakespeare.

(Then:)

JOE: What a stupid thing to say. What a silly thing to say, Merle . . . What does that mean?

BERNIE: Joe . . .

JOE: It just sounds clever. But what does it mean?

PEGGY *(What she's been thinking)*: Maybe someone else should play Olivia, Joe. Not me.

MERLE: Peggy.

PEGGY: We can't even afford to hire a sitter.

COLLEEN: You'll be great. Won't she, Joe?

JOE: I already told her that, Colleen.

(Then:)

We can afford a sitter.

(Mary returns with the whiskey and glasses.)

PEGGY: I'll have a whiskey.

(As the whiskey is poured:)

JOE: The Board of Education called me this morning—this was after our meeting.

MERLE: You didn't tell me this.

JOE: They're not going to send any more kids to our shows this winter. So they won't be paying for any more student matinees.

MERLE: That's most of our winter's budget. When were you going to tell us this?

(Then:)

DAVID: This is funny. You want to hear something funny? Who wants to hear something funny?

BERNIE: I need something funny.

MERLE: Me too.

DAVID: Joe's big trailer?

JOE: What about it?

MERLE: What? What are you talking about?

JOE: What's wrong with our trailer?

DAVID *(To Merle)*: The flatbed we have sitting now collapsed in the park?

MERLE: You mean our stage. It's not 'collapsed.'

PEGGY: It looks collapsed.

DAVID: It can't be moved. The wheels don't . . . Pretty much the definition of collapsed. I was telling Mary this. She said I should tell all of you. That it's funny. *(To Mary)* His garbage truck.

MARY: It is very funny.

DAVID: Robertson told me how Joe— *(To Mary)* Did John tell you this?

MARY: I haven't seen John. I told you that. I don't see him.

DAVID *(To the women)*: How Joe got that trailer into the park this week . . . As if he didn't have enough on his mind . . . .

JOE: It's good to be busy. *(To Peggy)* We need to be busy.

BERNIE: This week?

PEGGY: I haven't heard this.

DAVID: John said Joe called him late at night and said, meet him at the entrance to the park.

(They are laughing.)

JOE: So? Why is this funny?

DAVID: So John goes and he's waiting, and then, there coming down Central Park West, he sees a big goddamn garbage truck. Guess who's driving this big garbage truck?

BERNIE: Joe!

JOE *(Over this)*: So what? Why is this funny?

DAVID: Joe's driving it. God knows where he got it. And attached to this garbage truck, pulling behind—is our stage.

BERNIE: Where the fuck did you get a garbage truck?

DAVID *(To Joe)*: Where the hell did you get it? *(To Bernie)* Robertson said he asked the same question and Joe won't answer.

JOE *(To Bernie)*: Why do you care? I needed a big truck.

DAVID: We don't know. He won't say. So Joe pulls into the park. And this is in the middle of the night.

BERNIE: Of course.

MERLE: This is legal?

DAVID: The park's closed for hours now. And a policeman on a horse is there. He sort of rides up to the garbage truck. What the hell is this? He must be thinking. And Joe, he just sort of—salutes the guy. And the cop says nothing, lets Joe drive right in. I guess the cop is thinking, if he's got a garbage truck dragging what looks like a big fucking stage, and he's saluting me, then this guy must know what he's doing . . . He must belong here.

(Then:)

JOE: We do—belong there. And I think we're all grown-ups here.

GLADYS: Don't listen to Stuart.

MERLE: To hell with him.

JOE: And I'm going to keep this going if I have to drag the damn thing to another state . . .

DAVID: What about Utah?

MERLE: I'll push it with you.

JOE *(Over this)*: If I have to pull that trailer with my goddamn teeth. If I have to charge some money? . . . So what? If I have to pass around a hat? Beg. I'll beg. I've begged. *(About Merle to Bernie)* We keep having the same conversation over and over and over . . . He doesn't listen!

MERLE: I listen, Joe. I just don't agree. Listening doesn't mean you have to agree.

JOE: It doesn't?

(Then:)

COLLEEN: I can just imagine the faces of those mothers, as it dawns on them: 'What happened to the swings . . . ?' 'Where's the sandbox?' 'Where the hell did this parking lot come from?'

MARY: You'd think the people who went to the restaurant could just take the subway. It's not much of a walk.

PEGGY: Good luck.

BERNIE: That'd be nice . . .

PEGGY: They don't.

(Lights fade.)

Scene 3

August, 1958. The temporary stage of the Shakespeare Festival, Belvedere lawn, Central Park. Night. Eleven P.M.

A short time after the final performance of Twelfth Night. *What remains of the last scene: two camp stools, a bench, a pewter pitcher and steins on the ground and prop leaves. Faintly, from another part of the park—folk dancing music; as well as other park sounds and distant traffic throughout.*

Joe sits on the bench and looks out into the empty 'theater.' John is entering with a small box for the prop leaves.

JOE: There you are, John.

JOHN: I just heard Carol saying, she thinks she now understands her 'fucking' part. *(As Carol)* 'And now I have to fucking stop.' Actors, Joe . . .

JOE: Actors . . . I know, John. Oh I know. I do think she got better.

JOHN: I need to pick up all these— *(Leaves, etc.)* They're borrowed.

JOE: You want help?

JOHN: I can do it.

JOE: I've been a stage manager, John.

JOHN: I know.

JOE *(Looking out)*: Look out there. I've been watching them. Why are they still here? The last two. And what the hell are they talking about so earnestly.

JOHN: Maybe the play.

JOE: No. No. I doubt that. Maybe—where to eat . . . Whether to walk or take the subway. Whose bed they're going to make love in.

JOHN: Joe, we have to figure out how we're going to get this goddamn stage out of here. And when do we do that? Tomorrow?

JOE: We'll do it tomorrow. I'll get a truck.

JOHN *(Smiles)*: Garbage truck?

JOE: If I have to.

JOHN: Good. I don't think we can store it anywhere. Can we? I've asked around . . . So we'll have to junk it for scrap. That seems a shame.

JOE: Don't be sentimental, John. It's just a bunch of wood. And next summer we'll get a real trailer and stage. And a truck. I have a friend in Queens. He'll give us a deal. It'll even be bigger. And one that doesn't bounce.

JOHN: Or feel like it'll flip over when you drag it around a corner . . .

JOE: Guaranteed. He's a friend.

JOHN: Good. That'll be a nice change.

JOE: Nice for you. For stage management. But this was okay. She served us well. She got us this far. Leave them *(The camp stools)* . . . I'll store them in our apartment. We own these, right? We didn't borrow them? The bench too. It's a nice bench.

JOHN: I'm not sure, Joe.

JOE: I think we own them.

(Gladys enters.)

GLADYS: Didn't rain. That would have been a real shame to cancel the last one.

JOE: Is Stuart still here? I know. He 'loved the show.' Thinks I'm now a wonderful director. That's what he says to my face. Is that what he told you?

GLADYS: Stuart said he loved it. *(To John)* You need help? *(He shakes his head, she continues)* He's taking some of the men down to the Cedar . . . He asked me to see if you'd come. Want to? I'm sure he'd be thrilled—

JOE: I'm going to go out with John. Buy him a drink. He's earned it. Just us stage managers. *(To John)* Is that all right? My friend here . . .

JOHN: I can't tonight, Joe—

GLADYS *(To John)*: Aren't you coming too? With Stuart. I think John's coming too, Joe.

JOHN: We all said we'd go . . . A lot of people are going. Not just— Come to the Cedar . . . I need to lock this stuff away. Lock up everything. Come with us to the Cedar . . . Come on. It'll be fun. Just the guys . . . Maybe I'll see you downtown. I'll save you a barstool.

JOE: Leave that last light on. I'll shut it off . . . Oh, and John, if Stuart offers you work, take it. Look after yourself.

JOHN: Do you mean that?

GLADYS: Of course he doesn't. He really doesn't. Goodnight, John.

JOHN: Night, Gladys. Joe. Thank god it didn't rain.

(John goes off with the props.)

JOE: I hope it does rain now, Gladys. I want to stand here in a big goddamn rainstorm.

GLADYS: Oh come on, Joe.

JOE: John's going to work for Stuart . . .

GLADYS: I know. And he knows you know. So that was mean. He can do both.

JOE: Sit down. Sit down . . . Do you know what Stuart's season is going to be? He told me. Has he told you?

GLADYS: I'm his wife. It wasn't his idea, Joe.

JOE: I thought he's the 'boss.' *Only* plays by—'Nobel winners.' That's just stupid. You need someone to give them a prize first before you have the guts to put on his play? I thought we are doing something different. Those our age . . . Us. Do something different. Or just try to. Let the Shuberts pander all they damn want . . . We'd win just by trying. Let the rich guys build their palaces of art. And lock the gates at night. This is supposed to be different, Gladys. Next I want to do *Antony and Cleopatra* with Colleen and George Scott.

GLADYS: That would get an audience.

JOE: And put all of Egypt and Rome on this stage.

GLADYS: The girls are going to Carol's . . . It's for Peggy.

JOE: I know.

BERNIE *(Off)*: Joe!! You son of a bitch!

(Bernie and Merle are entering.)

JOE: Bernie. What the hell are you doing here? I didn't know . . . *(Grabs Bernie)* You said you couldn't come!

BERNIE: I snuck out . . . My assistant does everything anyway . . . How could I miss . . . ?

MERLE: I didn't tell you Bernie was here.

JOE *(Hugging)*: Bernie . . . Bernie. You saw the show? Go, Gladys. Enjoy yourselves. You all deserve to. Now I'm fine. Now I'm fine. Go. I know you'd be the last to leave this sinking ship. And god bless you for that.

BERNIE *(Trying to make a joke)*: What 'sinking ship'? Where the hell's the sinking ship? It was really great tonight.

JOE: You thought so?

MERLE *(Looking out)*: Who's out there?

JOE *(Explaining)*: I've decided those two are discussing: his place or hers . . . Or maybe just thinking about it. By now they've forgotten the play ever happened.

BERNIE: Of course.

JOE: It doesn't last long.

(They all look out.)

BERNIE: It's only a play.

JOE: Don't stare.

MERLE: They're waving . . .

(They wave.)

JOE *(Quietly)*: Glad you enjoyed the show . . . Thank you for coming.

GLADYS: I don't have to go if you need me . . .

JOE: No. No. I'm sure. I'm all right. I'm with my friends.

GLADYS: Goodnight. Merle. Bernie . . . So glad you came. Goodnight . . .

(She hurries off.)

JOE: It's been hard on her. Really hard. Divided loyalties . . . That's hard.

BERNIE: And with an asshole for a husband.

JOE: Now be fair, Bernie. Then on second thought . . .

MERLE: He's a friend. I got Bernie a ticket. He doesn't like to stand in line. And I told him he'd have had to get here very early. It's always a very long line.

JOE: Stop it. Don't try to cheer me up, Merle.

(Then:)

I'm sorry. If I were standing up here in a storm, I think I'd want you with me, Merle. By my side . . . *(Smiles)*

MERLE: Stuart's here . . .

JOE: Say something else . . . Sit. Sit. They're a little uncomfortable. *(The camp stools)* I tried to tell the actors, I don't want anyone sitting for too long; keep the show moving . . . Still—they complained. They were cheap, I think. Or we got them from somewhere . . .

BERNIE: What's next, Joe?

JOE: Colleen and Scott are going to do *Antony and Cleo* in the winter.

MERLE: You didn't tell me that. A reading?

JOE: It'll bring in some money. That's to get the ball rolling again. After our hiatus. I suspect— I'm not going to waste our time and money on just a reading, Merle.

BERNIE: I meant *you*, Joe.

JOE: What?

BERNIE: What are you doing next? After tonight. Right now. While on 'hiatus.'

MERLE: Should we go someplace? Have a drink . . . Bernie, when's your train—?

BERNIE: I'm staying in town tonight.

MERLE: Joe?

JOE: Bernie, I'm going to Cleveland, to judge some acting contest for the playhouse there. Some Ford Foundation thing. I'm angling for a grant from them . . . I thought this might . . . They give money to directors, don't they? I'm a director. They'll probably give me one of those grants.

MERLE: Why wouldn't they? *(To Bernie)* Right? They should.

JOE: Ten thousand bucks.

MERLE: Wow. *(A joke)* I should be a director.

BERNIE *(Trying to make a joke)*: If you get it maybe you can pay me back that loan for the O'Casey.

JOE: That wasn't a goddamn loan, Bernie. *(To Merle, 'incredulous')* Bernie put his own money into a show. *(Continues)* Then we're going out to Peggy's family. Her dad hasn't seen the kid yet.

BERNIE: A vacation, good.

MERLE: Recharge the batteries.

JOE: They're paying our way there . . .

(They all look out at the empty audience, not knowing what to say.)

The kids are gone. We've been forgotten . . .

(Peggy entering and seeing Bernie:)

PEGGY: Bernie?!

BERNIE: I'm here! I'm made it.

PEGGY: Joe, Bernie came. Joe said you couldn't come.

BERNIE: I wouldn't have missed it for anything.

PEGGY *(Hugging him)*: Joe, Bernie.

JOE: I know.

BERNIE: I loved it. I loved.

PEGGY: What are you three doing out here?

PEGGY: Bernie?!

MERLE: I don't know, what are we doing?

PEGGY: Everyone's still back there, changing, Bernie. Go and say hi, if they knew you were here and you didn't . . .

BERNIE: They don't care about me.

PEGGY: Bull. You've worked with half of them. Go. Go . . . They'll be hurt if you don't.

BERNIE: Okay. Okay. You were really great tonight. Such a beautiful Olivia.

PEGGY: Thank you . . . Thanks, Bernie. That means a lot.

JOE: Her last show. Her 'last time onstage.'

BERNIE: Don't say that. Why do you say that?

JOE: That what she says . . . You try and argue with her . . . I've given up. So has Merle.

MERLE *(To Bernie)*: Come on, let's go say hello. Get that over with. We'll be right back. We're not going away.

BERNIE: You're quitting? She's quitting?

MERLE: And don't go anywhere without us. You're stuck with us . . . Come on. Come on. And try and just say hi, you don't have to schmooze with everyone . . .

(Bernie and Merle are gone.)

PEGGY: They're good friends.

JOE: Did you hear what Bernie just said? "A beautiful Olivia." I whole-heartedly agree.

PEGGY: I heard a friend say a nice thing. A very nice thing. I appreciate that. I do. There's a party. For me . . . Isn't that sweet? Just the girls. You think the sitter will be okay with that?

JOE: She'll be okay.

PEGGY: She's probably asleep by now.

JOE: Peggy, sit down. Sit down and look out there . . . I keep looking out there. But then maybe you need to go off with the girls—

PEGGY: No. No, I have time.

(She will sit.)

JOE: Stuart went backstage. Did you see him? Did he say anything to you?

PEGGY: He didn't say anything.

JOE: I'm sorry. To hell with him.

PEGGY: I mean anything bad. He was a gentleman. A friend.

JOE: Who waited until the last night.

PEGGY: What did he say to you?

JOE: Stuart wanted to give me a few notes. To 'help' me the next time. 'If there is a next time,' he said. 'Let's hope there is a next time,' he said. How he too finds directing hard. That it's always best to ignore the critics. He held back from pointing out that Atkinson actually wished the show had been directed by Stuart Vaughan. But I could see that in his face. He wanted to—

COLLEEN *(Entering)*: Peggy? I'm ready to go to Carol's. I'm supposed to bring things. It's sort of a potluck. I just learned this. I have to find someplace that's open. I brought your things.

(Hands Peggy her purse, etc.)

PEGGY: I don't have anything to bring.

COLLEEN: Not you. Tonight you don't have to bring anything. This is your night.

JOE: Go. Don't keep Colleen and the girls waiting . . .

COLLEEN: Joe, she's worried about staying out late, because of the sitter. I keep telling her—tonight she can stay out as late as she wants . . . I'm right, aren't I?

JOE: You're right, Colleen.

PEGGY: Colleen, could you give me a minute? Or I can just meet you at Carol's. I know where it is . . . I'm coming. I will come. I promise.

COLLEEN: I'll wait. A nice show tonight, Joe. And thank god it didn't rain. We were lucky.

(She goes.
Folk dancing music in the distance, and distant traffic.)

PEGGY: I'm sorry about Stuart . . .

JOE: What the hell. Doesn't matter. It's finished.

(Then:)

PEGGY: Putting on my makeup tonight, I kept thinking of those late nights in Clurman's class? . . . How special was that? Everyone having put in a day at their job. Jobs they hated. Me too, I worked. I hated it. Somehow that made it even better. Made you appreciate it even more. And it wasn't about trying to *be* anything. Become 'someone.' Not really. Not for me. Maybe sometimes I got caught up in that stuff . . . But not really . . . *(Smiles to herself)*

Though look at George and Colleen. Good for them. They were in that class.

JOE: You're just as good as George and Colleen.

PEGGY: Just as we were beginning tonight, and I was about to come onstage—given everything, I'd figured I'd have a lot of emotions to hold back and 'be professional'—but as I was about to enter, I heard myself, say to myself: 'I am so grateful.'

(He looks at her.)

For having had this, Joe. Throughout the show, I kept trying not to peek out there. I hope you didn't notice. 'Grateful.'

(Then:)

Given the chance to just to *do* it. And have it not be about anything else, but—doing it. Does that sound silly? Am I making any sense?

JOE: Yes . . .

PEGGY: What I think I love most about— This . . . The festival here. Why I'm grateful. It's obviously not been about money. *(Laughs)* It certainly hasn't been about that. So you feel that acting here— Ask anyone. Any of us. That's what we talk about in the dressing room—how and why it has been worth it to fight the rain, the sirens— *(Gestures off)* —the folk dancing festivals—

JOE: Is that what that is?

PEGGY: I didn't even hear it during the show. Did you? *(Another)* The planes from Idyllwild.

JOE: I've asked them to fix that. They can easily reroute—

PEGGY: I'm sure they listened. The accordion competitions—?

JOE: Oh god, I remember . . .

PEGGY: It's a very special thing. *I* think. When it's not about paying. Of course it is for them. *(The audience)* But not just for them, but for us too. I think they then look at us, at the show, differently. It's not like we *owe* them something. It's not about *owing*. Or them *buying* anything. And that doesn't mean they're not expecting or even demanding— But in a different way, Joe. Like—talking to someone. That person you're talking to doesn't owe you an answer, but it is only fair to expect a response because you're *there*, you're listening, you've spent *time*. It's—person to person, human to human being. Today, I suppose that just sounds naive . . .

(She looks at him.)

JOE: I hope not. Anyway, we only did free because we had to in the other park . . .

PEGGY: I know. I know that. Things happen that you can't plan for. There are good surprises too.

THE WOMEN *(Off)*: Peggy! Come on. Peggy!

PEGGY: I have to go, Joe.

JOE: Go. Go have fun with the girls.

PEGGY: And you with the boys.

(Then:)

We met in a play. *(About him)* The stage manager and understudy. *(About herself)* And one of the whores. A clean-cut whore from Utah. National company. *Salesman.* Remember when you went on as Happy . . . ?

JOE: I try to forget.

PEGGY: The saddest looking Happy I ever saw.

JOE: I was scared. I'm no actor. I'm too shy. Still your parents really liked us . . .

PEGGY: Joe, they liked me. *(Smiles)* Night.

(She goes.)

JOE: Goodnight.

(A plane is heard overhead.)

(Calls after her) I am going to get those rerouted!!!

(Joe is alone.
    Folk dancing festival continues off; traffic; voices passing by,
etc.
    Then: Bernie and Merle enter.)

MERLE: All the women are going off together. To a party. Just—
    the women. What do you want to do, Joe?
JOE: And the men with Stuart. What do you want to do?
BERNIE: I don't know. We don't have to go anywhere. We can sit
    here. What do you want to do? Merle wants to go to a bar.
MERLE: It's going to rain.
JOE: The party's for Peggy.
BERNIE: Peggy okay?
JOE: It's what she now wants.
BERNIE: Look what I've got . . . *(Takes out a small flask)* Who
    needs to go to a bar? Who wants a drink? Joe?
JOE *(Taking it)*: Thank you.
BERNIE: I find that *(The flask)* helps on the New Haven line.
    Makes the seats a little less hard.
JOE: You are something, Bernie . . . You always think you can
    make anything better . . .

(Drinks and hands the flask to Merle.)

BERNIE: So you're going to Utah.
JOE: And Utah is a very interesting place. I go fishing. I . . . I
    think that's it. Fishing. But a nice clean place. My father-
    in-law's a good man.
BERNIE: He's the politician.
JOE: He has been. He's a lot more than that.
MERLE: Did you know this, Bernie? Joe once helped on one of
    his campaigns.

BERNIE: I didn't know. That I would have liked to have seen. Joe Papp in Utah knocking on doors—

JOE: For about a day . . . A nice place. Nice. 'Nice.'

BERNIE: Merle, I've known Joe for years now. And for almost all of that time, I had no idea he was a Jew too. 'Papp.' I thought it was Greek. I even asked Joe once—what part of Greece are your folks from?

MERLE: You're kidding.

JOE *(To Bernie)*: What did I say?

BERNIE: Athens. Probably the only Greek place you knew . . .

JOE: Bernie, did you really like the play tonight? My direction? I know you'll be honest.

BERNIE *(Hesitates)*: Didn't rain. I thought it might. That would have been terrible. I mean—your last night.

JOE: At least you're honest. We'll be back next summer, Bernie.

BERNIE: I know. I meant . . .

MERLE *(To say something)*: Who's the better stage manager? I'm looking at you two and wondering that. What do you think?

JOE: Don't try and make us happy, Merle. You don't always have to play the fool. How much did we get in our buckets tonight? *(To Bernie)* I decided just to beg.

BERNIE: Fuck Moses.

MERLE: I said we'd count it later.

BERNIE *(Looks out)*: What a beautiful place to do theater. Fucking Stratford is a fucking barn. You know the theater you used on the East River?

JOE: In that park. Yeah. What about it?

BERNIE: Merle was just telling me— How did it come up? I don't know. Anyway he was telling me: do you know why that was built? In that park? Who it was built for?

(Joe looks at Merle.)

MERLE: I just learned this.

BERNIE: How that came into being? I mean it just sits there now mostly empty.

JOE: How? I don't know.

BERNIE *(To Merle)*: I don't know how you know all this.

MERLE: I hang out with gossips. I'm a press rep.

BERNIE: Himself. Mr. Moses had that amphitheater built—to kiss the ass of Governor Smith.

JOE: What do you mean?

MERLE: When he was a kid, Smith— He grew up in that neighborhood. And it seems he always had these dreams of being an actor. But he never could afford the price of a ticket to a theater. So that was Moses' gift to Governor Al Smith. *(Incredible)* A theater . . .

BERNIE: How are you going to store this—[stage]?

JOE: We're just going to junk it. Get a better one next year.

MERLE: Joe has a friend—

BERNIE: Like the friend you had who built you the last trailer? *(To Merle)* I rode that once. Never again. Every time you turned a fucking corner—

JOE: Another friend. In Queens. He has a car shop—

BERNIE *(Over this)*: If you paid more than a few bucks, Joe, you might—

JOE: I don't have any money, Bernie.

(Mary appears.)

MARY: Good, you haven't left . . .

JOE: You're still here, Mary. Our biggest fan.
How many times did you see it? *She* loved it.

MARY: Some of the women are still getting dressed. And I've been delegated to invite you gentlemen to our girl party.

MERLE: If it's a girl party . . .

JOE *(Same time)*: I don't think so . . .

MARY: We heard you were still here. And we suddenly realized—how boring it would be with only us girls. *(Smiles)* Come on. Please, you'll come won't you?

BERNIE: We'll think about it, Mary. It's at Carol's? I know where that is. We're going to sit out here a little longer.

MERLE: Mary just got a part in George's play this fall.

BERNIE: Good for you, Mary.

MARY: Colleen got me the audition.

MERLE: Joe is stage managing.

BERNIE: I didn't know that. We'll see you at Carol's.

MARY: You're not just saying that, are you, Bernie?

BERNIE: We're just saying it, Mary. And please tell Gladys to stop worrying about us.

MARY: You do know it's going to rain.

MERLE: Oh we know.

(She goes.)

BERNIE: She still with David?

MERLE: She has got him so fucked up . . .

JOE: Stuart wanted to cast her. Remember? She'd have been good.

MERLE: She probably would have . . . Yeah . . .

(Then:)

JOE: Watching tonight, and seeing Stuart here, I didn't care what anyone in that audience thought of the show—only goddamn Stuart. What is wrong with me? I wanted to show him. Petty? Sure. And so when he gave me that 'smile' and . . . You know. You can imagine how he said . . .

MERLE: He's not a bad guy.

BERNIE: No . . .

JOE *(Looking out into the dark)*: No.

BERNIE: Forget it . . .

JOE: I kept having this dream these past few weeks. While rehearsing *Twelfth Night*. I suddenly find myself in a place—I don't know where. I'm lost. A beautiful beautiful place. Trees. Grass. A lake. Like this. It's like this park. Where the city noise is just 'over there.' It's all mixed together. All one thing. Like here. But I know I've never been here before. I'm lost. Then someone comes by—I first think it's you, Merle, but then he turns and it's not you. I don't recognize him. And I say, excuse me, sir, where am I? He turns to me and says, "This is Illyria . . ."

BERNIE: Like in the play. He's been rehearsing too hard, Merle. He needs a break.

MERLE: I agree. And fortunately, now he has one . . .

JOE: Looked just like this.

BERNIE *(Looking off)*: I really liked—what was that place called where we worked?

MERLE: When?

BERNIE: The three of us. With the O'Casey—the one Joe still owes me the money for. It was in the west forties. What was it called? I was trying to remember.

JOE AND MERLE *(They work it out together)*: Yugoslav-American Center, or culture or something or other—

JOE: Not the forties. It was higher than that.

BERNIE: I don't hear anybody doing anything there anymore.

MERLE: It got knocked down, Bernie. They knocked it down.

JOE: Oh, that's a shame. You can do plays in a place like that. It felt nice. Like people had lived there. It felt like people. You weren't putting things on some pedestal. Just life.

BERNIE: Like a park.

JOE: Like a park. Full of people. I sometimes wonder if this is what the parks people are afraid of. And their rich friends. Of us sitting in the dark together. Maybe they just want to keep us apart. Keep us in 'our place.'

BERNIE *(Sings quietly)*:
 Bellow goodbye to the buggerin' lot come out
 To bow down the head 'n' bend down the knee to the
 bee . . .

JOE *(To Bernie)*: You have a terrible Irish accent, Bernie . . . .

MERLE: That wasn't his Irish accent, that's his singing voice.

BERNIE: You know we're probably really lucky, Merle. Imagine what Joe would be like, if they hadn't kept him in his place.

JOE: What do you mean by that?

BERNIE: There'd be no living with him. Wouldn't be just 'Joe Papp presents.'

MERLE *(Laughing)*: Oh no!

JOE: Come on. Come on.

MERLE: It'd be 'Joe Papp presents the world!'

BERNIE: Presents the sun! And the moon!

JOE *(Over their laughter)*: I don't think that's true. I don't think I'm like that all.

MERLE *(To 'Bernie')*: You know Joe always hates it when I refer to the festival and say 'we.'

JOE: That is not true, Merle. And what would be wrong with that anyway? *(To Bernie)* He's just a goddamn press rep.

MERLE: Who works for free . . .

JOE: Even that's more than you're worth.

MERLE: Maybe I should be paying you, Joe. Like his 'students'! *(Smiles)*

JOE: That was a good idea. Why didn't I think of that?

BERNIE *(Over this)*: What students? What??

JOE: Kids need to learn—

MERLE: You don't know about this? Bernie doesn't know about—?

JOE: It's nothing—an experiment.

MERLE: Joe made a deal with NYU for some students—work for us and they get credit. We charged them $195—

BERNIE: To work for you? You got them to pay you?

JOE *(Defensive)*: They got credits, Bernie.

BERNIE: $195??

MERLE: We limited it to thirty.

JOE: So they'd get enough attention.

BERNIE: How many signed up—?

MERLE: Four.

JOE: It wasn't worth it . . . More trouble than it was worth.

(Merle takes a swig from the flask.)

MERLE: Bernie, he's got me to write a release. About next season.

JOE: A draft. It's a draft. Everything's not set yet.

MERLE *(Over this)*: 'Everything'? All the wonderful shows we're going to do. Excuse me, that 'Joe Papp' is going to present. *(To Joe)* I hadn't known about *Antony and Cleopatra*. I'll have to add that in . . . Have you asked Colleen and George? Should I announce it as a full production or just a reading?

JOE *(Again)*: I'm not going to waste my time with just a reading, Merle.

MERLE *(Shrugs)*: I'll add it in.

(About the press release:)

'James Cagney in *Comedy of Errors*.' 'Katherine Hepburn in *Taming of the Shrew*.'

BERNIE: I'd like to see that. I've worked with her. She'd be good as Kate. Except for the ending. I don't think she'd do that.

MERLE: It's just to get people's attention. And then, Joe says, once you've got them interested and maybe they start to give you a little money then—'Oh, I'm sorry, Miss Hepburn's got a movie, Jimmy's changed his mind, he can't learn lines and so you end up with I don't know—Staats Cotsworth, he's just as good.' 'Even better.' 'More stage experience.'

BERNIE *(Joining in)*: 'Why didn't we think of him first?'

(Laughter.)

MERLE: And then damn it—

BERNIE, MERLE AND JOE *(The punch line)*: 'Then *he* gets a movie!'

(Laughter.
Silence.
They drink.)

BERNIE: Should we go to the girls' party? We could.

JOE: I think tonight should be about sitting with two friends, on a stage, in the park. A castle behind us. And even a lake.

(Looks up.)

And it's not even raining. Not yet.

BERNIE: I think any minute.

MERLE: I think I felt a drop. These seats are really uncomfortable. Your poor actors.

BERNIE: What did they build on what was our Yugoslav-American whatever center? Or culture . . . Whatever it was called. Do we know?

MERLE: You don't know?

BERNIE: No.

JOE: I don't know. What?

BERNIE: What did they build?

MERLE: They knocked down that whole goddamn neighborhood. Everything else around it. A jazz club I loved. Restaurants. One day they just called it a 'slum,' named it 'a slum,' and then just tore it all down.

BERNIE: For what?

MERLE: Joe knows.

JOE: Is that where that was? It was there? We were there?

BERNIE: What?

JOE: Shit. They're building it now. Right?

(Merle nods.)

Their 'Palace of Art,' Bernie. The Palace of Art. *(To Merle)* Everything about that phrase is wrong. Including the 'of.'

MERLE *(To Joe)*: You know I didn't know that it's not even named for *Abraham* Lincoln—some other Lincoln.

JOE: I didn't know that either.

MERLE: Probably some rich guy, 'Lincoln.'

BERNIE: Makes sense.

JOE *(To Bernie)*: Did you happen to see this week's *Time* magazine?

BERNIE: No. What?

JOE: Don't people read in Connecticut, Merle?

MERLE: They're going to knock down Carnegie too—'oh we don't need that anymore.' 'Not with . . . our new palace . . .'

JOE: Because of the palace.

MERLE *(To Joe)*: Did you see the picture of what they're going to build there?

JOE: In *Life*. *(Nods)* All red, Bernie. Looks like a giant cheese scraper. I'll show you. You won't believe it. It'll make you sick.

MERLE: And it'll sit three, four stories off the goddamn sidewalk. So—far away from *'the scary'* street . . .

BERNIE: We need more mothers with fucking strollers . . .

MERLE: Yeah. We do . . . We do. Good idea.

BERNIE *(Over this)*: They haven't carved up Washington Square yet.

MERLE: Not yet.

JOE *(Suddenly shouts)*: It's our fucking city too!!

(It starts to rain.)

BERNIE *(Quietly)*: Hear that, rich people?

MERLE: It's raining. *(To Joe)* That's your fault, Joe. Moses must have heard you.

BERNIE: And Moses makes it rain?

JOE: That's what he seems to think . . .

MERLE: It's raining.

JOE: I'm not going anywhere.

(Then:)

(Sings)
　　When that I was and a little tiny boy,
　　With hey, ho, the wind and the rain . . .

I didn't like what David did with this. He's a good composer, but . . .

BERNIE: Good and cheap.

JOE: No. He's good. But *this* should be simple . . .

(Sings)
> A foolish thing was but a toy,
> For the rain it raineth every day.

BERNIE *(Sings quietly)*:
> But when I came to man's estate,
> With hey, ho, the wind and the rain,

MERLE: You know the words.

JOE *(Explaining why)*: He's a stage manager.

BERNIE: We did *Twelfth Night* last season too.

JOE: Remember? They wouldn't give us their damn costumes either?

MERLE: I remember . . .

BERNIE *(Sings)*:
> 'Gainst knaves and thieves men shut their gate,
> For the rain it raineth every day.

(Merle who doesn't know it, joins in with the refrains.)

JOE AND BERNIE:
> But when I came, alas, to wive.

ALL THREE:
> With hey, ho the wind and the rain.

(Roll of thunder.)

MERLE: And goodnight to you, Mr. Moses . . .

JOE AND BERNIE:
> By swaggering could I never thrive,

ALL THREE:
> For the rain it raineth every day.

BERNIE: Should we go?

(Thunder.)

JOE: I don't want to go anywhere. I just want to stay here.

(Sings)
> But when I came unto my beds,
> With hey, ho, the wind and the rain,

JOE AND BERNIE:
> With tosspots still had drunken heads,

ALL THREE:
> For the rain it raineth every day . . .

END OF PLAY

AUTHOR'S NOTES

In researching the play, I consulted numerous books, archives, newspapers, etc. These are the most important books: Stuart W. Little's *Enter Joseph Papp*; Helen Epstein's superb *Joe Papp: An American Life*; Kenneth Turan and Joseph Papp's *Free For All: Joe Papp, The Public, and the Greatest Theater Story Ever Told*; Arthur Gelb's *City Room*; Stuart Vaughan's *A Possible Theatre*; Robert Simonson's *The Gentleman Press Agent: Fifty Years in the Theatrical Trenches with Merle Debuskey*; Robert A. Caro's *The Power Broker: Robert Moses and the Fall of New York*; Anthony Flint's *Wrestling with Moses: How Jane Jacobs Took on New York's Master Builder and Transformed the American City*; Alice Sparberg Alexiou's *Jane Jacobs: Urban Visionary*; three books by Jane Jacobs, her masterpiece, *The Death and Life of Great American Cities*, *The Economy of Cities* and *Dark Age Ahead*.

Articles included: J. M. Flagler's "Gentles All" ("Onward and Upward with the Arts," *New Yorker*, August 31, 1957); Leticia Kent's "Jane Jacobs, An Oral History Interview" (Toronto, October 1997) and numerous reviews and articles from the *New York Times*, the *New York Herald Tribune* and the *Village Voice*.

The press releases for 1958 of the New York City Parks Department proved helpful. The archives of the New York Shakespeare Festival (Billy Rose Theatre Division, New York Public Library for the Performing Arts) proved essential.

The song Bernie and Joe sing at the beginning of Scene 2 is from *Within the Gates* by Sean O'Casey.

Richard Nelson
Rhinebeck, New York